Reflections on the Book of Enoch

An Accessory to the Book of Enoch

By Tiffany Root & Kirk VandeGuchte

All quotes from The Book of Enoch come from The Complete Book of Enoch by Dr. Jay Winter (2015), translated from the original Ethiopic manuscript and logically organized, unless otherwise indicated. These references are indicated by the book number, chapter number, and verse number(s).

Introduction

This is the time for revealing and understanding the mysteries of God that have been hidden for centuries and millennia. It is the time of God's Great Reset where things hidden are being revealed, where lies are broken, truth is told, and justice prevails. It is the time when history books will be rewritten for those who desire to know the truth. It is the time where the great apostles of God arise and bring the revelation of Jesus Christ, with the help of their prophets, which is the foundation of the true church. It is the time for the Bride of Christ to be found without spot or wrinkle, to be truly washed by the water of the Word – the LORD Jesus Himself.

These end times are the times Enoch wrote about, the people he wrote to, they are the people the Prophet Daniel wrote to, and this is the time where the church takes over all the mountains of influence in the world and brings the Lordship of Jesus Christ to the nations. Some call it the Millennial Reign. It is the time when the two witnesses in John's Revelation of Jesus Christ, the Apostles and Prophets who only follow the voice of the LORD, rise up and declare: **"The kingdoms of this world have become the kingdoms of our Lord and of His Christ, and He shall reign forever and ever!"** (Revelation 11:15) Amen.

Table of Contents

Chapter 1:
Enoch the Scribe of Righteousness

---◆◇◆---

Enoch was born the seventh generation from Adam. His father was Jared, and his son Methuselah is known as the man who lived the longest (so far) on earth. Enoch is also the great-grandfather of Noah. And he is one of the patriarchs in Jesus' lineage. Enoch is known as a man of great faith. He pleased God so much, God took him rather than letting him die. As it is written,

By faith Enoch was taken away so that he did not see death, "and was not found, because God had taken him;" for before he was taken he had this testimony, that he pleased God. But without faith it is impossible to please Him, for he who comes to God must believe that He is, and that He is a rewarder of those who diligently seek Him. (Hebrews 11:5-6)

Other than that, Enoch's name only comes up in the Bible for the purposes of the lineage of Abraham and when Jude quotes something that Enoch wrote. However, there are many references to the writings of Enoch throughout the scriptures that do not specifically name Enoch. Those references can be found in the Book of Enoch, also referred to as 1 Enoch.

In the Book of Enoch, Enoch is described as a scribe of righteousness, and we can find conversations with angels, the Lord, and the Nephilim (offspring of angels and humans).

Enoch records visions and prophecies regarding the end times, and he brings words of judgment against the fallen angels. He transcribed what was going on in his day, and that history was read by those who wrote the scriptures we find in the Bible. Jesus Himself even read Enoch. We know this because He referenced Enoch's writings when speaking to the Sadducees. The writers of the Bible knew who Enoch was, and they were familiar with what he had written. He was actually a very important person in biblical history.

Enoch was so important that of the 16 people named in the Faith Hall of Fame chapter of the Bible (Hebrews 11), which include: Abel, Noah, Abraham, Sarah, Isaac, Jacob, Joseph, Moses, Rahab, Gideon, Barak, Samson, Jephthah, David, and Samuel, Enoch was one of them. Now think of how many people are named in the Bible. There are a lot! But Enoch is the first one recorded as having faith after Abel died. He was very unique in his day, and even mediated between God and the Watcher Angels (referred to as sons of God in Genesis 6).

The Lord took Enoch because he was a righteous man, a man of faith, and God wanted to spare him from death. This doesn't mean, however, that others who died were not righteous. Those close to Enoch, like his son Methuselah, were righteous. Obviously, Enoch's great-grandson Noah was righteous. But most people were evil as evidenced when God wiped mankind off the face of the earth and started over with Noah and his family.

Again, this doesn't mean Enoch was more righteous than those in Christ now, or even that what was happening in Enoch's day was worse than things are right now. However, we are establishing that he was a righteous man. God and angels called Enoch a scribe of righteousness.

And I Enoch was blessing the Lord of Majesty and the King of the ages, and lo! the Watchers called me, Enoch the scribe, and said to me: "Enoch, thou scribe of righteousness, ... (1:4:23)

Enoch was not righteous because he never did anything wrong. He was righteous because of his faith. Just as God credited righteousness to Abraham because of his faith, so He did for Enoch. And so He does for each of us. No one has ever been righteous because of their works of the flesh, but because of their faith in God.

Having established the righteousness of Enoch because of his faith, we must also note that Enoch fulfilled his mission on earth. He was to transcribe his visions and conversations with the Lord and the angels. He did so. Had there been more for him to do on earth, the Lord would not have taken him. But his mission was complete, and the Lord desired to spare him from death. That's the thing with God. He can do as He pleases. We like to put Him in a box and use scriptures like "it's appointed once for a man to die," so that we can say Enoch has to come back and die. But he doesn't. He fulfilled his mission, God was pleased with him, and God took him. God can do that.

Additionally, Enoch testifies that he wanted to go to heaven, and God granted him his request. He writes,

"There [in heaven] I wished to dwell, and my spirit longed for that dwelling place, and there heretofore hath been my portion. For so has it been established concerning me before the Lord of Spirits" (2:1:20).

There is a lot we can learn from this man, Enoch, who walked with God, talked with angels, frequently visited heaven, and eventually was taken by God to heaven without experiencing death. Through the writings of Enoch, we will see the judgment of the Lord, the righteousness of the Lord, the glory of the Lord, and the exaltation of the Son of God.

Chapter 2:
Books of Enoch & Their Translations

Enoch testifies of Jesus and the victory of the righteous in the earth throughout his writings, which is typical of prophecy. Some writings ascribed to Enoch are not his, but a good portion of 1 Enoch are not only Enoch's writings, but they are inspired by the Holy Spirit and when read with the Holy Spirit are useful for edification, exhortation, inspiration, a witness of the truth, and training in righteousness.

The reason we are being led by the Spirit of Christ to write about the Book of Enoch is because Enoch testifies to Jesus Christ. Father is always interested in talking about His Son. We will find as we go through the Book of Enoch that not only do Enoch's writings exalt Jesus, but they were written with this generation in mind. Enoch was writing for a generation in the future, and that generation is us.

The Lord is a Revealer, and in these end times He is revealing the things that have been hidden for a long time. As He does, Jesus will be lifted high because truth will be proclaimed. Praise God!

Currently, we have no record of anyone writing before Enoch. Of course, the sources from the world do not recognize that Enoch wrote anything and so they come up with other ideas of the oldest writing. However, if there is writing before Enoch, we do not know about it yet.

There are three books currently attributed to Enoch. We say currently because we believe more manuscripts will be found that are actually written by Enoch. As far as what we have right now, the first book has five books in it and is the one most commonly read and used. It is called 1 Enoch, Ethiopic Enoch, or simply, the Book of Enoch. Most translations of 1 Enoch break it up into 108 chapters that are compiled within five books. These five books are not to be confused with 1 Enoch, 2 Enoch, and 3 Enoch. Instead, the Book of Enoch is comprised of five books called 1 Enoch.

The books titled 2 Enoch and 3 Enoch do not have the witness of the Holy Spirit. Scholars too question their authenticity as being authored by Enoch. In other words, most people do not believe Enoch wrote 2 Enoch or 3 Enoch. As an overview, 2 Enoch is also called The Slavonic Enoch or the Book of the Secrets of Enoch. Depending which translation you read, it follows Enoch through seven or ten heavens and relates a history of creation. It has many things in it that do not align with correct doctrine.

The rabbinic Enoch is also known as 3 Enoch. It is thought that a rabbi wrote this. This book not only does not bear witness of the Holy Spirit, but it actually feels demonic. For example, Enoch is made into an angel. That's not only wrong, but it would be a downgrade for someone in Christ to be made into an angel.

Because these works do not bear the witness of the Holy Spirit, we will not be writing about them. We'll stick with the Book of Enoch, otherwise known as 1 Enoch.

The Book of Enoch has been used by the Ethiopian Orthodox Tewahedo Church for centuries. It may also have been used by other Christian and Jewish groups, but overall has not been in normal circulation for Christians.

There are several versions of the Book of Enoch available for reading, some you need to purchase and some you can find online for free. Some translators or editors add portions of the Book of Noah or the Book of Giants to their translations. Some add 2 Enoch and 3 Enoch to their edition of 1 Enoch. It can be very confusing.

The Lord has said that without the Holy Spirit we're guaranteed to be deceived because He's the Spirit of Truth who leads us into all truth. Therefore, the first step in deciding which version of the Book of Enoch to read is to make sure you have the Holy Spirit and that what you are reading, you are reading with Him. You should always ask the Holy Spirit to read with you.

If you have the Holy Spirit, then ask Him if you should read the Book of Enoch, and then which version. One of your choices will be the version by R. H. Charles, which is probably the most common version. He breaks the Book of Enoch up into 108 chapters, with the last few chapters being portions of the Book of Noah. We have found that there is the witness of the Holy Spirit up through Chapter 59 in this version of the Book of Enoch. After that, the witness of the Holy Spirit is sporadic.

Another popular version of the Book of Enoch is by Dr. Jay Winter. His version can be downloaded for free from the internet. He includes history with his version, which is very helpful. He also compiles his version in an easier to read format than Charles does. For whatever reason, he does not include chapters 53 and 103 from Charles' version. Chapter 53 is a good chapter, but not necessary. When reading the version by Winter, the Holy Spirit lifts after Book 3, Chapter 3, verse 14. From this point, Winters inserts portions of the Book of Noah and then goes back to the Book of Enoch later. However, as noted with Charles' version, the witness of the Holy Spirit is mostly lacking in the rest of the book.

Another possible version you could read is a paraphrase by Michael Fickess. He paraphrases chapters 1 through 59 of Charles' book. The paraphrase does help with understanding Charles' translation. And it's convenient to have just the portion that is definitely inspired by the Holy Spirit. Fickess also includes a topical index in the back, which some may find helpful. However, he includes footnotes with his own theological thoughts, which are not always correct according to the Holy Spirit. These footnotes can detract from what the Holy Spirit is saying. It's similar to footnotes in the Bible that, depending on who wrote them, will sway the reader to one theological interpretation or another of the scripture.

There are more versions of the Book of Enoch than those we have listed, so just ask the Holy Spirit which one you should read. But no matter which version you use, read it with the Holy Spirit. That's the most important thing. And do not approach the reading of the Book of Enoch as a book study. Approach it like you would any other scripture: to see what God is saying and to know Him better.

In this book, we will not be discussing what is written in 2 Enoch and 3 Enoch. We only want to focus on what is inspired by the Holy Spirit. Therefore, when we refer to the Book of Enoch, we are referring to the first 59 chapters as divided by R.H. Charles, which would correspond with Book 1 and Book 2 through Chapter 3 verse 14 as translated by Dr. Jay Winter.

While the Book of Enoch contains what Enoch has written, it does not appear to have been compiled by him. Instead, it looks like perhaps one of Enoch's descendants made a compilation of his writings with a few narration notes, and that is what we have today. As time goes on and God reveals more of what has been hidden for many generations, we will likely find out more specific details regarding the compilation of the Book of Enoch.

The Book of Enoch starts out with these words:

The words of the blessing of Enoch, wherewith he blessed the elect and righteous, who will be living in the days of tribulation, when all the wicked and godless are to be removed. And Enoch, a righteous man whose eyes were opened by God took up his parable and said, "I saw the vision of the Holy One in the heavens, which the angels showed me, and from them I heard everything, and from them I understood as I saw, but not for this generation, but for a remote one which is for to come." (1:1:1-2)

As you can see, the book starts out in the third person, but then changes to first person when it is something Enoch actually wrote. Another example would be this verse:

Before these things Enoch was hidden, and no one of the children of men knew where he was hidden, and where he abode, and what had become of him. And his activities had to do with the Watchers, and his days were with the holy ones. (1:4:22)

Again, this is written in third person, explaining what happened to Enoch.

There are also a few verses that indicate the book was compiled of Enoch's writings after God took Enoch, like when it records that God sent the angel Uriel to speak to Noah about preparing for the flood.

Then said the Most High, the Holy and Great One spake, and sent Uriel to the son of Lamech and said to him, "Go to Noah and tell him in my name 'Hide thyself!' and reveal to him the end that is approaching, that the whole earth will be destroyed, and a deluge is about to come upon the whole earth, and will destroy all that is on it. And now instruct him that he may escape and his seed may be preserved for all the generations of the world." (1:4:9)

Enoch was taken by God before Noah was born, and this was not written as though Enoch was prophesying about the angel talking to Noah, though Enoch did prophesy about the flood.

Here is one last example for our purposes showing that Enoch did not compile his writings in the Book of Enoch as we have them today, but someone else did it for him.

The second vision which he saw, the vision of wisdom, which Enoch the son of Jared, the son of Mahalaleel, the son of Cainan, the son of Enos, the son of Seth, the son of Adam, saw. (2:1:1)

These are a few examples that show Enoch did write what is contained in the Book of Enoch, but it was compiled by someone else. However, the greatest reason we believe this is true is because that is what the Holy Spirit is telling us. The Lord says that the people who pieced together the Book of Enoch were not being nefarious, but it was a little embellished here and there and may have lost something in the translations from language to language. However, the first part of the book should not be questioned. Therefore, the Book of Enoch, while not compiled by him, does include his writings, is accurate, and does exalt Jesus.

Moving onto what's contained in 1 Enoch, or the Book of Enoch. In this book are five books. They cover topics like the Watcher angels and their giant offspring (the Nephilim); parables; a study of the sun, moon, and stars; visions of heaven; part of the Book of Noah; and some wisdom and revelation shared by Enoch. Depending on which version you read, these topics are divided up in various ways. For example, as stated previously, the most common way to read Enoch is probably the translation by R.H. Charles. This translation divides the Book of Enoch into 108 chapters. Personally, I found this very confusing. Then the Lord led me to a different version translated by Dr. Jay Winter. In his own words, his version is "Translated from the original Ethiopic manuscript and logically organized." It is definitely organized in a more readable way.

In all of this, what we're interested in is Jesus. We must keep Him as our focus. When we read Enoch, we must be asking, "Is Jesus preeminent?" We will find that parts of 1 Enoch have Jesus as being preeminent. For example, the Second Parable in 1 Enoch reads in part:

And there I saw One who had a head of days, and His head was white like wool, and with Him was another being whose countenance had the appearance of a man, and his face was full of graciousness, like one of the holy angels. And I asked the angel who went with me and showed me all the hidden things, concerning the Son of Man, who he was, and whence he was, and why he went with the Head

of Days. And he answered and said unto me: "This is the Son of Man who hath righteousness. With whom dwelleth righteousness, and who reveals all the treasures of that which is hidden." (2:2:7-9a)

Passages like this exalt Jesus, show He is preeminent, and bear witness of the Holy Spirit. These are the types of passages we will focus on during our travels through the Book of Enoch.

Chapter 3:
Are the Writings of Enoch Scripture?

The term "scripture" refers to holy writings. For Christians, these would be writings that are inspired by the Holy Spirit. Most often scriptures are written by Apostles, Prophets, or those closely associated with either of those offices, like the doctor, Luke. The reason God does this is because apostles and prophets are tasked with laying the foundation of the church, which is built on the revelation of Jesus Christ. Therefore, when these offices are submitted to the Lord, their writings reveal Jesus and carry the authority of their offices.

We will find as all things are revealed that there have been many scriptures hidden from us for the purposes of deception. The enemy does not want the testimony of Jesus Christ available to the church or the world. Nor does he want the church to understand that we have victory over the powers of darkness. We are <u>not</u> waiting to be raptured out of anything. We are here to bring the Kingdom of Heaven to earth as we make disciples of the nations. (See *The Revelation of Jesus Christ and the End Times* for more on end times theology: https://a.co/d/8AzgkWq)

During the time of Christ on earth, the Book of Enoch was considered scripture, meaning inspired by the Holy Spirit. Jude quotes a portion of Enoch when he writes,

Now Enoch, the seventh from Adam, prophesied about these men also, saying, "Behold, the Lord comes with ten thousands of His saints [holy ones], to execute judgment on all, to convict all who are ungodly among them of all their ungodly deeds which they have committed in an ungodly way, and of all the harsh things which ungodly sinners have spoken against Him." (14-15)

In order for Jude to quote Enoch, he had to know what Enoch wrote, which means he read the Book of Enoch. And Jude gives credence to the validity of the Book of Enoch by declaring what Enoch prophesied was happening at the time Jude wrote his portion of scripture. If what Jude was quoting was validified as true prophecy, then it means that the prophecy was inspired by the Holy Spirit. It was scripture.

Besides Jude's outright quote of Enoch, there have been found to be over one hundred phrases in the New Testament that can be traced back to the Book of Enoch. In other words, the writers of the New Testament believed that at least parts of the Book of Enoch were scripture.

However, the greatest reason we should believe that the Book of Enoch, or at least part of what we have now as the Book of Enoch, is scripture is because Jesus called it scripture. There is no higher authority than Jesus. When Jesus was speaking with the Sadducees, He told them that they did not know the scriptures, nor the power of God (Matthew 22:29). He then went on to tell them that in the resurrection, people are like angels in the respect that they are not given in marriage. This truth comes from the Book of Enoch. It is not found in the scriptures that are contained in the Bible as we know it. The Lord told the Watcher angels through the Prophet Enoch:

But you were formerly spiritual, living the eternal life, and immortal for all generations of the world. And therefore I have not appointed wives for you; for as for the spiritual ones of the heaven, in heaven is their dwelling. (1:5:27)

Therefore, since Jesus referred to the Book of Enoch as scripture, or at least a part of the Book of Enoch as scripture, it is acceptable for us to call it scripture as well.

Having established that at least part of 1 Enoch is scripture, let's look at some of the references to the Book of Enoch found in the Bible. There are many references in the Bible that can be traced back to the Book of Enoch. There are not any that reference 2 and 3 Enoch, but there are many that reference 1 Enoch.

To begin with, Jesus taught many things that can also be found in the Book of Enoch. For example, Jesus said, **"Blessed are the meek, For they shall inherit the earth"** (Matthew 5:5). And Enoch wrote, **"But for the elect there shall be light and joy and peace, and they shall inherit the earth"** (1:2:14). Isaiah too prophesies about the saints inheriting the earth.

I will bring forth descendants from Jacob,
And from Judah an heir of My mountains;
My elect shall inherit it,

And My servants shall dwell there. (Isaiah 65:9)

Besides the inherent theme that those in Christ will inherit the earth, notice the use of the term "elect." This term is used throughout scripture to speak of those who are in Christ. Jesus uses it in Matthew 24 twice (verses 24 & 31), and He uses it again when He says, **"And shall God not avenge His** own elect who cry out day and night to Him, though He bears long with them?" (Luke 18:7)

The Apostle Paul also uses the term "elect" throughout his writings. For example, in Romans 8:31, he writes, **"Who shall bring a charge against God's elect? It is God who justifies."** And again in Romans 11:7, **"What then? Israel has not obtained what it seeks; but the elect have obtained it, and the rest were blinded."**

Additionally, Peter and John also use the term "elect" when referencing the saints in Christ. For example: **"She who is in Babylon, elect together with you, greets you; and so does Mark my son"** (1 Peter 5:13). And **"The children of your elect sister greet you. Amen"** (2 John 1:13).

Why is this important? The term "elect" comes from the Book of Enoch. Jesus is referred to as the Elect One. And those who follow Jesus are called the elect ones. This is irrefutable. Here are just two verses from the Book of Enoch, but the terms "Elect One" and "elect ones" are found throughout 1 Enoch.

On that day Mine Elect One shall sit on the throne of glory and shall try their works, and their places of rest shall be innumerable. And their souls shall grow strong within them when they see Mine Elect Ones. And those who have called upon My glorious name: Then will I cause Mine Elect One to dwell among them. And I will transform the heaven and make it an eternal blessing and light and I will transform the earth and make it a blessing: and I will cause Mine Elect Ones to dwell upon it: But the sinners and evil−doers shall not set foot thereon. (1:2:3-5)

Father Himself spoke from heaven calling Jesus "The Elect One" in Luke 9:35 (**"This is My beloved Son. Hear Him!"**). The translators evidently changed it to agree with the wording found in Matthew and Mark, but that is not what it says in the original Greek in Luke. Originally, the Greek read, "ho eklelegmenos," which literally means the "elect one." Therefore, Luke 9:35 should read: **"This is My Son, the Elect One. Hear Him!"**

It's also interesting to note that Jesus references a prominent theme in the Book of Enoch when He teaches the Parable of the Wheat and the Tares. In this teaching, Jesus makes it clear that the evil ones will be removed, and the righteous will remain to bring the Kingdom of Heaven to earth. The very first verse in the book of Enoch states this same theme. It says:

The words of the blessing of Enoch, wherewith he blessed the elect and righteous, who will be living in the days of tribulation, when all the wicked and godless are to be removed. (1:1:1)

Mount Sinai is also first mentioned in the Book of Enoch. It says, **"And the eternal God will tread upon the earth, even on Mount Sinai and will appear in the strength of His might from the heaven of heavens"** (1:1:4).

Mount Sinai is mentioned throughout scripture, and indeed God came down and met with Moses there.

"And let them be ready for the third day. For on the third day the LORD will come down upon Mount Sinai in the sight of all the people" ... **Now Mount Sinai was completely in smoke, because the LORD descended upon it in fire. Its smoke ascended like**

the smoke of a furnace, and the whole mountain quaked greatly ... Then the LORD came down upon Mount Sinai, on the top of the mountain. And the LORD called Moses to the top of the mountain, and Moses went up. (Exodus 19:11, 18, 20)

The Book of Enoch also speaks of Jesus forgiving sins and of eternal life.

And all the righteous shall rejoice, and there shall be forgiveness of sins, and every mercy and peace and forbearance ... And their lives shall be increased in peace, and the years of their joy shall be multiplied in eternal gladness and peace all the days of their life (1:2:11, 17).

Enoch even speaks of the four winds, which can also be found in Jeremiah, Ezekiel, Daniel, Zechariah, Matthew, Mark, and Revelation. And there are too many more references to write about in this book.

The point is that the Book of Enoch was widely read by those who wrote what is now included in the Bible. Jesus was familiar with Enoch, and so were the other writers. The same terminology is used throughout the Bible as was used by Enoch. The same concepts were understood. And most importantly, the same Spirit, who raised Jesus from the dead and dwells in us who believe inspired at least a good portion of what we find in the Book of Enoch.

So, why wasn't the Book of Enoch included in canon scripture? Well, canon scripture means the writings that councils of men decided at different periods of time after Jesus' ascension should be circulated and used within the church. Over time there have been many councils who would determine which

Hebrew writings should be included in the Old Testament and which Greek or Aramaic writings should be included in the New Testament.

The Old Testament seemed easier for these councils to agree on because those prophecies, psalms, and various writings had been in circulation and taught by rabbis for centuries. Supposedly, these councils used Jesus' words in Luke 24:44 to determine what kinds of books should be included in the Old Testament. Jesus said,

"These are the words which I spoke to you while I was still with you, that all things mut be fulfilled which were written in the Law of Moses and the Prophets and the Psalms concerning Me."

The Law, Prophets, and Psalms all prophesied of Jesus. Therefore, the various councils took books they deemed written by prophets and included them in the Old Testament. However, the Book of Enoch was also used for centuries and testifies of Jesus, yet it was excluded.

The New Testament was apparently more difficult for the various councils to come to agreement on, even though the first church didn't seem to have an issue understanding what constituted scripture. For example, Paul deemed Luke's gospel as scripture when he quoted it in 1 Timothy 5:18. He writes, **"For the Scripture says, 'You shall not muzzle an ox while it treads out the grain,' and 'The laborer is worthy of his wages.'"** These two scripture quotes come from Deuteronomy 25:4 and Luke 10:7 respectively.

Additionally, Peter recognized what Paul was writing as scripture while Paul was writing it. Peter writes,

[O]ur beloved brother Paul ... has written to you ... speaking ... these things, in which are some things hard to understand, which untaught and unstable people twist to their own destruction, as they do also the rest of the Scriptures (2 Peter 3:15-16).

It was evidently a common practice to pass around the letters from the apostles to the various churches. Therefore, these letters were widely accepted by the church as inspired by the Holy Spirit. When the various councils decided to canonize certain writings, they mostly took into account what was being circulated among the churches. They also looked at whether an apostle or someone close to an apostle had written the document and if it was consistent with the teaching of the rest of what they already considered scripture.

The term "canon" means

1. A law, or rule of doctrine or discipline, enacted by a council and confirmed by the pope or the sovereign; a decision, regulation, code, or constitution made by ecclesiastical authority.

2. The collection of books received as genuine Holy Scriptures ... (The GNU version of the Collaborative International Dictionary of English)

To put it in simpler terms, those who canonized the Bible were attempting to make an authoritative book for the church to use to regulate moral guidelines and doctrine.

Obviously, a main reason men put together a book and called it "canonized" was to control what Christians were reading. But there may have been good reasons too, like it's easier to have one book of inspired writings, rather than a hundred separate books to carry around.

Besides councils that attempted to canonize scripture, there were individuals who sought to put together a book that would be used as "the" Bible for the church. William Tyndale was one of the first to do so in the English language. By 1534 he had translated the entire New Testament and Genesis through 2 Chronicles before he was imprisoned for his work. When Mary I took over the throne of England, she outlawed Protestantism. Therefore, many Protestant scholars fled to Geneva, where they translated what became known as the Geneva Bible, which relied heavily on Tyndale's Bible. Since Tyndale's Bible was not completed, the Geneva Bible became the first English version to be translated in its entirety from the original languages of Hebrew, Greek, and Aramaic.

King James I did not like the Geneva Bible because there were passages he thought could be used to undermine his authority as king, and there were passages and notes that showed the church government was not as it should be. He also stroked his ego a bit by changing Jesus' brother Jacob's name to James. Now we read the book of James instead of the book of Jacob. For these and other reasons, King James I set up a council of men to translate what we consider the "Bible" today into English. When this new Bible named after King James I was completed, it didn't sell well. People preferred the Geneva Bible. So, James outlawed all other versions of the Bible and made his the only one.

The books included in these versions and most of the Protestant Bibles thereafter do not include the apocryphal books. In the introduction to Dr. Jay Winter's translation of the Book of Enoch, David Chariot writes,

"The Enochian writings, in addition to many other writings that were excluded (or lost) from the Bible (i.e. the Book of Tobit, Esdras, etc.) were widely recognized by many of the early church fathers as 'Apocryphal' writings. The term 'apocryphal' is derived from the Greek word meaning 'hidden' or 'secret.' Originally, the import of the term may have been complimentary in that the term was applied to sacred books whose contents were too exalted to be made available to the general public."

Nowadays, however, the term apocryphal carries mostly a negative connotation. Many believe the books found under the category apocryphal do not belong in the Bible because they do not believe they are inspired by the Holy Spirit. This attitude is not reserved for just the Protestant denominations either.

The Catholic church rejected the Book of Enoch in the 4th Century B.C. However, if you have an understanding of Catholicism, you can see why they would do this. Their government requires there to be men at the top who go to God on behalf of the people on the bottom. They could not allow that Enoch, a regular man, could talk to angels, ascend to heaven, or speak to God because the Catholic church is the go-between for God and men. The very fact that they conducted their masses in Latin (which most of the "regular people" could not understand) until the late 1900's proves this point.

When researching why the Book of Enoch was not included in the Bible, I came across the words "scholars" and "theologians" repeatedly. Somehow, we believe that the smartest people are the ones who make the best decisions. However, not only is that not true, but it is giving preference to the Tree of the

Knowledge of Good and Evil over the Tree of Life. As Paul writes,

But we speak the wisdom of God in a mystery, the hidden wisdom which God ordained before the ages for our glory ... But God has revealed them [the mysteries] **to us through His Spirit. For the Spirit searches all things, yes, the deep things of God.** (1 Corinthians 2:7, 10)

Only those with the Spirit of God understand the mysteries of God. Yet it was scholars and theologians who decided what to include in the Bible. In all my research, I've yet to come across a record of anyone testifying that they heard the Holy Spirit tell them to make a book of approved scriptures Christians should read or if that were the case, what those approved scriptures should be. That should concern us. If we are led by the Spirit of God, why do we give credence to what those who are not led by the Spirit of God tell us is right or is wrong?

Those who did not want the Book of Enoch included in the Bible may have had good reason, but was it following the Holy Spirit? Is the Book of Enoch not inspired by God? Is it not referred to in the other books of the Bible repeatedly? Didn't Jesus Himself say it was scripture? Didn't the Apostle Jude (originally Judah) quote directly from Enoch? If Enoch was widely read in Jesus' day by those who were filled with the Holy Spirit, why would we be told we shouldn't read it? Why would it be deliberately taken out of circulation and suppressed?

There are many reasons why those who put together the Bible did not want Enoch in it. For starters, what is translated by R.H. Charles includes some literature that does not bear the witness of the Holy Spirit. In other words, part of the Book of Enoch is not inspired by God. However, the first part, chapters 1 – 59 do bear witness of the Holy Spirit. So, to give some credit to the compliers of the Bible, they may have excluded the Book of Enoch because the last half of it is not entirely inspired by God.

And yet, there are so many reasons the Book of Enoch should be considered scripture. Many of those reasons we already covered. Besides the references by Jesus and the first church, it is obvious after reading 1 Enoch that chapters 1 through 59 as divided by R.H. Charles was common reading for Jews. For example, there is reference to a Watcher angel in Daniel 4:13-23. These are the type of angels of whom 200 were judged in Enoch's day. There is also a section that parallels Genesis 6:1-4. In the Book of Enoch, it reads:

And it came to pass when the children of men had multiplied that in those days were born unto them beautiful and comely daughters. And the angels, the children of heaven, saw and lusted after them, and said to one another: "Come, let us choose us wives from among the children of men and beget us children." (1:3:1-2)

In Genesis, it reads:

Now it came to pass, when men began to multiply on the face of the earth, and daughters were born to them, that the sons of God saw the daughters of men, that they were beautiful; and they took wives for themselves of all whom they chose. (Genesis 6:1-2)

Besides this example from Genesis and Daniel, there are references in Haggai, Zechariah, Malachi, Isaiah, the Psalms, and many more books found in the Bible that bear a great resemblance to verses found in the Book of Enoch. It doesn't take much deducing to realize that the writers of the Old Testament were familiar with the writings of Enoch. It also is obvious that the same Spirit that inspired the writers in the Old Testament inspired the writer of the Book of Enoch.

However, after the time of Jesus on earth, a crusade began to get rid of the Book of Enoch. The Christian "fathers" who lived in the second century B.C. were offended by the writings regarding fallen angels. And the Jewish rabbis were offended by clear references to Jesus. Both started to condemn the Book of Enoch, and at least one rabbi pronounced a curse on those who believed Enoch's writings. Eventually, the Book of Enoch fell into such disfavor with church and synagogue leaders that it seemingly disappeared for a thousand years.

In these last days, the Lord is having us look at the Book of Enoch because the prophecies found therein are very similar to the prophecies the Lord has given to His prophets today regarding the judgment of the wicked and the blessing of the righteous. So, despite the offense that the Book of Enoch causes for those who are caught up in religion, for those of us with the Holy Spirit, we will see that the Book of Enoch is yet another witness of the resurrected Jesus Christ.

It is amazing that the Book of Enoch survived all this time. The Book of Enoch records that Enoch told his son Methuselah to keep his writings and pass them down for a future generation. Therefore, Methuselah would certainly have given those manuscripts to Noah to preserve on the Ark. The Book of Jasher records that Shem took what was written that was preserved on the Ark and taught Abraham. (The Lord says the Book of Jasher is historical but embellished in parts.) From

Abraham the Israelites would have received whatever writings Noah would have preserved on the Ark. This is evidenced even by Moses' writings that reflect some of what is found in the first part of the Book of Enoch.

Some question why Moses did not elaborate more on the Watcher angels and the Nephilim if the Book of Enoch is true. Well, why would Moses feel it necessary to include all the details found in the Book of Enoch when the writings of Enoch were accessible to any who desired to read them?

After the time of Jesus on earth, the Book of Enoch was used by some Christians and Jews despite being discarded by the majority of Christian and Jewish leaders. The Ethiopic Church preserved the Book of Enoch, and this was discovered by an English-speaking man from Scotland named James Bruce in the late 1700's. Bruce brought three copies from Ethiopia back to Europe where someone eventually translated the Book of Enoch into English.

Many years later in 1947, some shepherds discovered caves near the Dead Sea in the Qumran area in which there were many jars filled with scrolls. Among these scrolls were fragments of at least ten Enoch manuscripts, as well as other texts not found in the Bible right alongside texts that are found in the Bible.

After Bruce brought back the Ethiopian Enoch manuscripts, many people had believed that the Book of Enoch must have been written after Christianity started. However, the discovery of copies of the Book of Enoch among the Dead Sea Scrolls proves that it was in existence previous to the life of Jesus on earth because the scrolls are dated as having been written/copied before Jesus' time on earth. And of course, the fact that Jesus refers to Enoch and calls it scripture, proves it was being read by the Jews of Jesus' day.

Interestingly, the Dead Sea is an unique area in which the atmosphere is very arid with low humidity, making it an excellent area in which to preserve ancient documents. The sea itself is called dead because it contains so much salt that not much can live in it, except microorganisms like fungi and algae. It's thought that Sodom and Gomorrah are at the bottom of the south side of the sea, and that makes some sense because Moses records that God rained sulfur and fire down on those cities. One can do much research regarding this, but for our purposes, the finding of the Dead Sea Scrolls just proves that the Book of Enoch was in existence before Christ and that it was widely read by Jews, which means also would have been widely read by Christians.

When men decided to canonize scripture, it is possible they had access to the Book of Enoch, but it's also very possible they did not because the Book of Enoch was not "found" in Ethiopia until after the earliest Bibles were put together. And yet, here we are today, over 5,000 years after Enoch walked the earth still talking about what he saw and wrote. Truly the Lord knows how to preserve his words spoken through His prophets despite what man tries to do to stop Him.

All of this goes to show that it was not God who put the Bible together. Instead, it was men. Man has always tried to take the place of the Holy Spirit. In determining what Christians can and cannot read, men have decided that people cannot follow the Holy Spirit for themselves. Yet, it is the Holy Spirit who leads us into all truth. His name is the Spirit of Truth after all!

Even so, people have fallen for the idea that somehow God Himself put the Bible together and determined this is what His followers must read. People have even called the Bible the word of God. It is not. Jesus is the Word of God. There are a lot more than words from God found in the Bible. There's also words of Satan and evil men and women recorded in the Bible. It's time to appreciate the Bible, but no longer allow it to be what we worship.

When we were asking the Lord about this topic, He spoke to us and said: *"I didn't sanction the assembly of the Bible. It was done apart from Me."*

Sanction means "Authoritative permission or approval that makes a course of action valid" (The American Heritage® Dictionary of the English Language, 5th Edition). This means God is saying that He did not give permission nor approval to the compilation of the Bible. In His eyes, it is not valid. It's another attempt of men to try to control what Christians read and believe. God did not give these men authority to make an "authorized version" of the Bible.

God did, however, inspire many writings over the millennia. Most of what you've read in your Bible is inspired by the Holy Spirit. It is scripture. But there are things that are not in your Bible that are also scripture. It's not that God is saying you shouldn't read what is found in your Bible. He's saying He didn't sanction the putting together of the Bible. Our faith is not based on a book, even what is labeled a "Holy" book. Our faith is in Christ, the living Word of God. Jesus must be preeminent in everything.

Therefore, use the scriptures as a witness to Jesus, but don't allow them to take His place. They are meant to testify of Jesus, not become Him.

Besides what is included in the Bible there are many other writings that have been inspired by the Holy Spirit. We'll see as we delve deeper into the Book of Enoch that a good portion of it bears the witness of the Holy Spirit. There are also other manuscripts that have been preserved over time that were written through inspiration of the Holy Spirit. Since we are in a time where truth is being revealed and what has been hidden is being brought to the light, we're sure we'll see many documents come forth that the enemy has worked to suppress because they bear testimony to Jesus. In fact, all inspired writings will in some way or another give testimony to the resurrected Son of God. Jesus said about the Holy Spirit: **"[W]hen the Helper comes, whom I shall send to you from the Father, the Spirit of truth who proceeds from the Father, He will testify of Me"** (John 15:26).

Holy Spirit testifies of Jesus. Therefore, prophecies written by prophets that have come via the Holy Spirit could be considered scripture. Doctrine written by apostles that have come via the Holy Spirit could be considered scripture. There is no rule that God has made that what is in the Bible is all the scripture there is in the world. In fact, His very nature shows this couldn't be true because Jesus is the Word of God and He continually speaks. How can words He spoke a long time ago be worth more than words He speaks today?

In a vision of the Holy City, Kirk saw himself representing the prophets who receive the word of God, which keeps things level and is the measure by which all things are measured/judged. In this same vision, I (Tiffany) am representing the apostles. I hold in my hand a book, which the Lord says represents correct doctrine. (See *The World and Church Prophecies: God's Great Reset* for this and other prophecies. https://a.co/d/6l7Q1jW)

Taking this into consideration, could a prophet writing by the Spirit of the Lord, not be writing scripture? Could an apostle writing doctrine for the church as she is led by the Spirit of Christ, not be writing scripture? Even the Apostle Peter said Paul was writing scripture while Paul was still alive. And Paul said Luke had written scripture, and Luke wasn't even an apostle or a prophet.

The Lord is saying the body of Christ has a stronghold, and it's called the Bible. He's breaking down the lies surrounding it. Yes, you can use the Bible. Yes, it is good to read, but only with the Holy Spirit. And yes, there is a lot more than what is written in the Bible that can be considered scripture. And yes, there will be even more written in the last days where the Spirit is poured out in even more power than ever before that will be considered scripture.

Another aspect to consider is that the ability to read is not required for one to be a disciple of Jesus Christ. There is no requirement from Jesus, who is the Head of His church, that someone be literate in order to be His disciple. However, Jesus did say that His church would be built on the revelation of Him, and that said revelation comes through His apostles and prophets. Wouldn't we therefore need to be able to read what the apostles and prophets write?

Not necessarily. Consider what Paul writes in Romans 10:13-15, 17.

For "whoever calls on the name of the LORD shall be saved." How then shall they call on Him in whom they have not believed? And how shall they believe in Him of whom they have not heard? And how shall they hear without a preacher? And how shall they preach unless they are sent? As it is written:

"How beautiful are the feet of those who preach the gospel of peace,

Who bring glad tidings of good things!"

So then faith comes by hearing, and hearing by the word of God.

The apostles and prophets are the foundation of the church, with Christ as the Cornerstone because the apostles and prophets bring revelation to the church. Jesus uses that revelation to build His church. Therefore, the message preached that Paul is referring to is the gospel of Jesus Christ. The gospel is the good news of the revelation of Jesus Christ. Paul is saying that someone needs to hear the message, not read it.

It is true that we can hear the Spirit of Christ speak to us *as we read*. But even then, we must be hearing. Many people read the Bible or other inspired written words, and they do not hear God as they read because they read it with their intellect. God is Spirit, and those who worship Him must worship in spirit and truth (John 4:24).

Therefore, while it may be very helpful to be able to read what the apostles and prophets write, it is not a requirement. It is required that we hear God. And hearing God will often come through His apostles and prophets. There are some things that

God will give to His church only through His apostles and prophets. Revelation for the church is one of those things. So, you will need to listen to the Lord's apostles and prophets even if you can't read.

In summary, men decided to put together a book of writings that included what they thought was appropriate for Christians to read and believe. Over the years, the Bible has been elevated to a place where people have put their faith in it and what it says over what the Lord says.

Even though what is found in the Bible may be good, it is not God. We cannot allow what is written in a book become our God. Jesus is King of kings and Lord of lords. When He speaks and it's written down, it's scripture. But that scripture is not Him. Our relationship must be with Him, not with a book. Therefore, be filled with the Holy Spirit and listen to His voice. Be led by Him, and you will not be led astray.

We'll end this chapter with a vision Kirk saw on April 7, 2023.

I (Kirk) was taken in the spirit to a large planet. As I approached it, I thought it was completely made out of scrolls. That's how it appeared to me. Then suddenly I was on a path through a wooded area. On the trail itself I noticed words. I studied them and realized that the words were from Jesus, words that He had spoken. I looked around and started to notice that everything here had words on it, all were words that Jesus spoke. I saw tree trunks with words, the leaves of the trees had words on them, everything had Jesus' spoken words on it!

I bent down and lifted a blade of grass. On the underside of this blade of grass, it said, "and God became flesh." I was thinking that I could spend forever here and not be able to read every word. It was beautiful, and also a bit intimidating because, well, having read the Bible and having taken in the words of Jesus in red letters, what I had read was less than a drop of water in the oceans of the earth. Untold numbers of Bibles could be written, and the word of God, Jesus, keeps speaking ... ("Planet of Scrolls Vision" found in *The World and Church Prophecies: God's Great Reset. https://a.co/d/6l7Q1jW*)

Chapter 4:
Summary of the Book of Enoch

B ecause the organization of the Book of Enoch as translated by Dr. Jay Winter is easily understandable, we'll use it as the translation we refer to as we do an overview of the Book of Enoch. Winter's translation seems to make more sense in how the different pieces are put together of the Book of Enoch, so it flows a bit better than other translations. Therefore, the chapters listed are according to his translation.

Book One, Chapter One in the Book of Enoch starts out saying, **"The words of the blessing of Enoch, wherewith he blessed the elect and righteous, who will be living in the days of tribulation, when all the wicked and godless are to be removed"** (1:1:1).

In other words, Enoch is writing to those of us who are living in the last days, those of us who are here to experience God's Great Reset as the tares are removed and the blessing of the Lord is poured out on the righteous. Enoch then goes on to praise the Lord and prophesy about the demise of the fallen Watcher angels, the coming of the Lord Jesus Christ, and the justice of God.

Chapter Two of Book One is all about Enoch's observations of creation and how God is praised in all of it. It's very reminiscent of Romans 1:20 in which Paul writes,

For since the creation of the world His invisible attributes are clearly seen, being understood by the things that are made, even His eternal power and Godhead, so that they are without excuse.

Even as Enoch praises God for His wisdom in creation, he flows right into rebuking the wicked for their hard-heartedness and then blessing the righteous and declaring they shall find forgiveness of sins, peace, joy, and eternal gladness.

Chapter Three of Book One is the beginning of Enoch's writings about the fallen Watcher angels, their giant sons, and all the evil they wrought upon the earth. He names the fallen Watcher angels who were "chiefs of tens," meaning each of these angels had authority over ten other angels who fell with them (1:3:3, 6). In all, there were 200 angels who fell in the manner of the Watcher angels by sleeping with women, begetting sons, and then teaching mankind how to do evil through witchcraft, war, astrology, etc.

The sons of the Watchers were "great giants" who ate all the food men could bring them, ate the men, sinned against the animals, ate each other, and drank blood. They were disgusting monsters, who were neither fully angels nor fully men. Therefore, Enoch ends this chapter by saying that **"as men perished, they cried, and their cry went up to heaven"** (1:3:14).

Is it any wonder that Moses introduces Noah's flood with a short explanation of the fallen angels, the women they married, and their giant sons? They had wrought such evil on the earth, a flood was needed to do a reset because God has not given the earth to angels or monsters. He's given it to men, and the reading of the Book of Enoch helps us understand this even more.

Chapter Four of the Book of Enoch begins with the archangels Michael, Uriel, Raphael, and Gabriel presenting themselves before God and asking Him what He would have them do to help mankind because of the evil being wrought on the earth through the fallen Watchers, their offspring, and the men who learned evil through them. The LORD answers the angels by giving them each tasks to do.

He begins by sending Uriel to Noah and instructing him to save himself and his family because of the coming deluge. Of note here is that Enoch was taken by God before Noah was born. Someone else is writing this part of the Book of Enoch, using mostly what Enoch saw and wrote, but some things are not from Enoch himself, like the beginning of Chapter four.

Next God instructs Raphael to bind Azazel, the leader of the fallen Watchers, under darkness and in pain until he's thrown into the lake of fire. The Lord says to Raphael,

"Bind Azazel hand and foot, and cast him into the darkness: and make an opening in the desert, which is in Dudael, and cast him therein. And place upon him rough and jagged rocks, and cover him with darkness, and let him abide there forever, and cover his face that he may not see light. And on the day of the great judgement he shall be cast into the fire." (1:4:10)

This of course corresponds with what Peter wrote, who was familiar with the writings of Enoch. Peter writes that **"God did not spare the angels who sinned, but cast them down to**

hell and delivered them into chains of darkness, to be reserved for judgment ..." (2 Peter 2:4).

After this, the LORD tells Gabriel to incite the giants to kill each other and sentences the giants (Nephilim) to live no longer than 500 years. It's interesting that this was considered a short lifespan. As we enter into God's Great Reset, we need to remember that the Holy Spirit gives life to our mortal bodies, and we should expect to live a long, long time. God does not strive with man anymore, so 120 years is not what we should expect. We should expect much, much longer. Perhaps even expect not to die!

Lastly, God tells Michael to bind Samlazaz and his associates who sinned with women until they are thrown in the lake of fire.

Then God says that when all the evil is destroyed, the righteous will beget thousands of children and live to old age in peace, and the earth will be blessed and righteous, and all people will worship God. Again, this is like what the LORD has prophesied regarding His Great Reset. He has said the tares would be removed, honesty would change the world, people would operate with good will toward men and God, and so much more.

We have so much good to look forward to. Even as we go over what was written in the past, let us keep our eyes on Jesus and look forward to what was prophesied so long ago that corroborates what has been prophesied in recent years.

Chapter Four then continues in Enoch's own words. Enoch relates that the angels came to him to give him a message to declare to the fallen Watcher angels. They say to Enoch, **"Say** to them: 'Ye have wrought great destruction on the earth and ye shall have no peace nor forgiveness of sin'" (1:4:24).

Enoch is also told to tell the fallen Watchers that they will see the destruction of their sons, and that they themselves will never obtain mercy or peace.

The fallen Watchers then ask Enoch to go before God on their behalf and petition God that they may be forgiven for what they have done. Enoch writes out their petition, and then Enoch goes away from them and reads the Watcher's petition until he falls asleep. As he is sleeping, the Lord gives him the answer to the petition.

Chapter Five begins with God's answer to the fallen Watcher angels. Enoch writes,

The book of the words of righteousness, and of the reprimand of the eternal Watchers in accordance with the command of the Holy Great One in that vision I saw in my sleep (1:5:1).

Enoch then recounts the judgment against the fallen Watchers and their sons. Interestingly, Enoch is judging angels according to what he has heard from the Lord. This is exactly what we who are in Christ will do as well. Paul writes, **"Do you not know that we shall judge angels? How much more, things that pertain to this life?"** (1 Corinthians 6:3)

The judgment Enoch relates to the Watchers begins with a rebuke from God, who Enoch saw on His throne. The Lord says, **"You should intercede for men, and not men for you"** (1:5:24). He goes on to render judgment against the fallen Watchers and their sons.

After this, Chapter Six recounts Enoch's travels through earth and heaven guided by angels. He's even shown a glimpse of hell, and he sees the judgment of the Watchers and the women with which they defiled themselves.

Lastly, in Chapter Seven, Enoch names the archangels and explains what they each have authority over. He has more visions of hell, he travels the earth, and he even sees the Garden of Righteousness, which would be the Garden of Eden. This chapter has a lot of symbolism, which we'll go into more later.

Book One of the Book of Enoch ends with a praise to the Lord:

And as often as I saw I blessed always the Lord of Glory, and I continued to bless the Lord of Glory who has wrought great and glorious wonders, to show the greatness of His work to the angels and to spirits and to men, that they might praise His work and all His creation: that they might see the work of His might and praise the great work of His hands and bless Him forever (1:7:68).

Book Two of the Book of Enoch consists of three parables. However, these are not parables like Jesus taught. These are more like allegories and visions Enoch saw.

The First Parable (Chapter One) comes after the angels take Enoch to various places in heaven and on earth. He sees what will happen when the wicked are driven from the earth. It's written by someone who records in third person what happened to Enoch, while also recording in first person what Enoch saw, spoke, and heard. For example, verse 11 reads, **"And in those days Enoch received books of zeal and wrath, and books of disquiet and expulsion"** (2:1:11). This

44

is third person, someone explaining what happened to Enoch. But two verses later, the writing is in first person, Enoch's point of view. It reads, **"And in those days a whirlwind carried me off from the earth, and set me down at the end of the heavens"** (2:1:13). The back and forth between first and third person continues throughout this parable.

Something else of interest in Chapter One is that Enoch asked to be taken to heaven. The way the account reads in Genesis does not give any clues about whether Enoch wanted to leave earth, knew he would leave earth, or anything else. It simply states that Enoch was not because God took him (Genesis 5:24). Junia expounds a bit on it in Hebrews 11:5 by saying Enoch pleased God because he had faith. See *Running Free Devotional Volume 2* for more information about who wrote the book of Hebrews.) But the Book of Enoch tells us a bit more. Enoch says,

"There [in heaven] I wished to dwell, and my spirit longed for that dwelling place, and there heretofore hath been my portion. For so has it been established concerning me before the Lord of Spirits." (2:1:20)

In other words, Enoch wanted to go to heaven, and the Lord established that he would be able to.

After this, Enoch sees some of the archangels praising the Lord, he sees various secrets of heaven, and he even sees **"mansions of the elect"** (2:1:36). We know, of course, that Jesus spoke of mansions in heaven too. He said, **"In My Father's house are many mansions; if it were not so, I would have told you. I go to prepare a place for you."** (John 14:2).

Enoch also sees wisdom personified as a woman. He writes,

Wisdom found no place where she might dwell, then a dwelling-place was assigned her in the heavens. Wisdom went forth to make her dwelling among the children of men and found no dwelling-place. Wisdom returned to her place and took her seat among the angels. (2:1:45-47)

Solomon too personified wisdom as a woman. He wrote much about wisdom in the Proverbs. For example,

Wisdom has built her house ...

She cries out from the highest places of the city,

"Whoever is simple, let him turn in here!" (Proverbs 9:1, 4)

It's interesting that even though we know Jesus has become for us wisdom from God (1 Corinthians 1:30), both Enoch and Solomon saw wisdom as a woman.

The parable ends with an angel explaining to Enoch that what he saw in his visions was **"their parabolic meaning"** (2:1:52). In other words, Enoch saw things that represented other things.

The Second Parable (Chapter Two) found in the Book of Enoch is rather amazing. It is all about Jesus. Enoch sees Jesus as preeminent, understands He is the Son of Man, the Elect One, the Anointed One, the Head of Days, and that He judges all things. He declares that it is Jesus who saves and that in Him is found all wisdom and counsel.

There are also references to hell giving up their dead for judgment and references to what it will be like on earth with the evil removed. For example:

In those days shall the mountains leap like rams and the hills also shall skip like lambs satisfied with milk, and the faces of the angels in heaven shall be lighted up with joy (2:2:44).

This is very much like Psalm 114:4, which reads: **"The mountains skipped like rams, The little hills like lambs."**

In addition to this, Enoch also prophesies about the coming flood. He writes,

And in those days shall punishment come from the Lord of Spirits, and He will open all the chambers of waters which are above the heavens, and of the fountains which are beneath the earth. And all the waters shall be joined with the waters: that which is above the heavens is the masculine, and the water which is beneath the earth is the feminine. And they shall destroy all who dwell on the earth and those who dwell under the ends of the heaven. And when they have recognized their unrighteousness which they have wrought on the earth, then by these shall they perish. (2:2:61-63)

Enoch ends this parable by prophesying about a coming battle between the righteous and the wicked which ends with Sheol (Hell) devouring the sinners **"in the presence of the elect"** (2:2:77). The righteous witnessing the justice of the Lord is a major theme throughout the Book of Enoch. And rightly so, because righteousness and justice are the foundation of God's throne, and He desires us to rejoice at His justice (Psalm 89:14).

Lastly, Enoch relates a third parable (Chapter Three) in which he begins by speaking of the blessings of God upon the righteous. After the first 14 verses of Chapter Three, the witness of the Holy Spirit lifts off this book. Verse 15 begins a portion from the Book of Noah, which isn't inspired by the Holy Spirit. Continuing on after that, there are verses here and there that do have the witness of the Holy Spirit, but they are scattered, and not necessary to read. What we do have from Enoch that has been inspired by the Holy Spirit agrees with scripture found in the Bible, and it does exalt Jesus.

Now, let's backtrack a little and discuss more in detail Chapter Seven of Book One. As mentioned previously, this chapter has a lot of symbolism. Here's a summary of verses 18-27:

Angels take Enoch to a mountain of hard rock in which there are four hollow places, which the Angel Raphael tells him are made for the souls of dead men waiting for the final judgment. Enoch sees one dead man crying out for justice. Raphael tells him that the man Enoch sees is Abel, and that he cries out until all of Cain's seed is annihilated from among mankind. Raphael goes on to explain that there are separations between the souls of the righteous and the wicked, and where the unrighteous dwell there is great pain. They are awaiting the final judgment.

When Cain killed Abel, the Lord said to Cain: **"What have you done? The voice of your brother's blood cries out to Me from the ground"** (Genesis 4:10). Abel was crying out for vengeance, as reiterated by Junia in Hebrews 12:24 where she writes that Jesus' blood **"speaks better things than that of Abel."** This would be better of course because Jesus' blood cries, "mercy" and mercy triumphs over judgment (James 2:13).

But wasn't Abel in heaven? Don't the righteous go to heaven? Why did Enoch see Abel in a hollow place in a mountain?

Rest assured, Abel is in heaven. He is a righteous man. He had faith and pleased God. The Lord says it's an allegory that the dead souls cry out for justice from various pits in the earth. The word "allegory" means: *the expression by means of symbolic fictional figures and actions of truths or generalizations about human existence or a symbolic representation* (Merriam Webster's Dictionary). Therefore, when Junia says Abel's blood cries out, she's referring to the allegory Enoch saw. (Remember that the writers of the Old and New Testaments were familiar with the writings of Enoch.) The other souls that Enoch saw were also either in heaven or in hell. Enoch was being shown symbolic representations to express various truths.

Enoch witnessed many things that were allegorical, as well as things that were parabolic. When he saw "lightnings" and "the stars of heaven" and how they had differing numbers of angels and they kept faith with each other, he asked the angel with him what he was seeing, and the angel replied: **"The Lord of Spirits hath showed thee their parabolic meaning: these are the names of the holy who dwell on the earth and believe in the name of the Lord of Spirits for ever and ever"** (2:1:52). What Enoch was actually seeing was a depiction of the saints on the earth. Joseph the son of Jacob also saw people as stars when he dreamed of his brothers and his parents bowing down to him. Parabolic is synonymous with allegorical. It's using a story or depiction of symbols to portray a truth.

When people get legalistic about words on a page, they run into trouble. This is why we need the Spirit of Truth to lead us into all truth. Jesus, Paul, and others "misquoted" and clearly changed the "original intent" of many passages of scripture as they were given revelation by the Holy Spirit. The Lord says, *"My Spirit is God, and My Spirit is not led by words on a page. He uses words on a page to lead."* Therefore, to think that we should take an allegory and make it literal is a big mistake.

There are only two places someone goes when they die: heaven or hell. Either a person is found to be in Christ or out of Him. There is no in-between.

While reading the Book of Enoch, be listening to the voice of the Holy Spirit and you will be edified. Enoch was a man of great faith, loved by God, and who loved God in return. As you read the Book of Enoch, you will recognize the voice of the Holy Spirit in much of what is written there.

Chapter 5:
Enoch's View of the End Times

Ideas of how the End Times will manifest abound. Theologians, pastors, prophets, and teachers all have their own thoughts and ideas of what things will be like. However, we follow Jesus, and so when we want to know what something will be like in the future, we need to look at Him. The End Times will be how Jesus said it will be, and Jesus paints a picture of justice and righteousness in which the evil ones are removed and the righteous inherit the earth as described in the Parable of the Wheat and the Tares.

Another parable He put forth to them, saying: "The Kingdom of heaven is like a man who sowed good seed in his field; but while men slept, his enemy came and sowed tares among the wheat and went his way. But when the grain had sprouted and produced a crop, then the tares also appeared. So the servants of the owner came and said to him, 'Sir, did you not sow good seed in your field? How then does it have tares?' He said to them, 'An enemy has done this.' The servants said to him, 'Do you want us then to go and gather them up?' But he said, 'No, lest while you gather up the tares you also uproot the wheat with them. Let both grow together until the harvest, and at the time of harvest I will say to the reapers, 'First gather together the tares and bind them in bundles to burn them, but gather the wheat into my barn.'" (Matthew 13:24-30)

Then Jesus sent the multitude away and went into the house. And His disciples came to Him, saying, "Explain to us the parable of the tares of the field." He answered and said to them: "He who sows the good seed is the Son of Man. The field is the world, the good seeds are the sons of the kingdom, but the tares are the sons of the wicked one. The enemy who sowed them is the devil, the harvest is the end of the age, and the reapers are the angels. Therefore as the tares are gathered and burned in the fire, so it will be at the end of this age. The Son of Man will send out His angels, and they will gather out of His kingdom all things that offend, and those who practice lawlessness, and will cast them into the furnace of fire. There will be wailing and gnashing of teeth. Then the righteous will shine forth as the sun in the kingdom of their Father. He who has ears to hear, let him hear!" (Matthew 13:36-43)

The words of Jesus are pretty clear. The tares are removed and the righteous shine in the kingdom of God.

Enoch's view of the End Times bears a striking resemblance to what Jesus taught. The very first verse of the Book of Enoch states: **The words of the blessing of Enoch, wherewith he blessed the elect and righteous, who will be living in the days of tribulation, when all the wicked and godless are to be removed** (1:1:1).

Sounds very much like the Parable of the Wheat and the Tares. There is a time of tribulation in which the wicked and godless are taken out, and the righteous remain to inherit the earth. As the Lord said, **"Blessed are the meek; for they shall inherit the earth"** (Matthew 5:5).

At another point, the Book of Enoch states,

In those days a change shall take place for the Holy and Elect, and the Light of Days shall abide upon them and glory and honor shall turn to the holy. On the day of affliction on which evil shall have been treasured up against the sinners. And the righteous shall be victorious in the name of the Lord of Spirits and He will cause the others to witness that they may repent and forgo the works of their hands. They shall have no honor through the name of the Lord of Spirits yet through His name shall they be saved, and the Lord of Spirits will have compassion on them for His compassion is great. (3:2:34-37)

This sounds like what the Lord said to us June 13, 2021.

"Behold, I Am holding the winnowing fork in My hand, and I Am separating the wheat from the chaff. I Am also separating the wheat from the tares! There will be no tares on My threshing floor says the Lord! The coming deception will clearly separate the wheat from the chaff! Only My wheat will be left, and the chaff will be blown away to another place, gathered, and burned, says the Lord. Likewise, My people shall be gathered together in an end times jubilee, but the end is not yet.

Rejoice, therefore, My people! I Am for you and not against you. I will bless you and I will remove from their place those who hate you! Look up! Your redemption is near! Amen." ("A Great Deception and an End Time Jubilee – Part 1" found in *The World and Church Prophecies: God's Great Reset.* https://a.co/d/8vNZOCH)

Enoch was seeing the days we are living in, and he was seeing the good that will come. We too have received many prophetic words of the great blessing coming to the righteous and the great judgment coming to the wicked.

Many people have interpreted the visions John saw in the book of Revelation as meaning that the world would become an increasingly horrible place to live in until the church just couldn't take it anymore, and they would need Jesus to rapture them out of it. This sort of eschatology twists some very obscure scriptures to make the case of a weak church needing rescue as the world goes to hell, while it ignores or misinterprets other scriptures that are very clear about a victorious church and a judgment against evil.

Lately, the Lord has taken hold of this lie of weakness, defeat, and escape and exposed it to the light. He has shown His people that victory is our destiny, not defeat. He has shown us that we are not meant to escape the world, but to take over and establish the kingdom of heaven in all areas of influence on the earth. He has reminded us that Jesus is the Head of His Church and Jesus never needs rescuing. He has made it clear that we are inheriting the earth, not working to bring His kingdom just so we can hand it over to the enemy. And He has shown us that the weak, defeatist, escapist mentality sees a big devil and a little God. That should not be.

As the Lord has brought prophecy after prophecy regarding His Great Reset, He has painted a picture of the future that is bright, filled with honesty, and where people actually follow His Spirit. He has repeatedly said the wicked would be removed during this time and that real justice would occur. He has said He is paying a recompense to the wicked and the righteous. He has said things like,

"Gold and silver shall be commonplace!

Food production shall increase as I bless the work of the farmers' hands.

The evil that held back and restrained shall be replaced with honesty and goodwill.

Socialism shall be viewed as the scourge on humanity that it really is! The people of the world will rise up against it, and they shall be successful.

My church – no not that one – MY church! It shall rise up, and the network of Apostles and Prophets shall be normalized.

A great purge of the filth in entertainment, the internet, and in government shall happen and anything less will not be accepted.

Schools shall be for learning!

Banks for saving!

Entertainment shall be fun again!

Work will become honorable!

Business shall be for the mutual benefit of the owner and the customer!

My churches shall be filled with My Spirit!" ("Righteous Will Reap a Harvest – Recompense Swift & Severe" – February 5, 2021 found in *The World and Church Prophecies: God's Great Reset*. https://a.co/d/8vNZOCH)

While Enoch did not see the future in this kind of detail, he did see the big picture where the wicked are removed and the righteous establish the kingdom of heaven on earth. Reading the Book of Enoch could help people establish in their hearts

God's plan for humanity. And reading the Book of Enoch would also bear witness that what the Lord has prophesied in the past several years regarding His Great Reset is truly what will happen.

Enoch admits that a good portion of what he was being shown was for a generation far into the future. It is written:

And Enoch, a righteous man whose eyes were opened by God took up his parable and said, "I saw the vision of the Holy One in the heavens, which the angels showed me, and from them I heard everything, and from them I understood as I saw, but not for this generation, but for a remote one which is for to come" (1:1:2).

The remote generation to come is the generation we are living in. Praise God!

Enoch's view of the End Times is in perfect alignment with what Jesus taught and with what the prophets of today have been shown.

(For more information on the End Times, see *The Revelation of Jesus Christ and the End Times:* https://a.co/d/9lk6fW6)

Chapter 6:
Angels

The Lord has told us repeatedly that He wants His people to learn how to work with angels in these end times. The Book of Enoch is a great resource for us regarding this topic because Enoch interacted with angels often when he was on the earth. For example, Enoch often spoke with the archangels who took him to various places on earth and in heaven, much of which is recorded in the Book of Enoch. In the Bible, archangels are referred to as chief princes (Daniel 10:13). Enoch also spoke with the fallen Watcher angels. We'll start by looking at the archangels.

These are the seven archangels according to what Enoch saw, and their varying assignments.

Uriel – His name means "God is my light," and Enoch saw him over the world and Tartarus (another name for the pit, hell, or even the chasm between heaven and hell). Interestingly, Kirk has conversed with Uriel and Jesus in visions regarding Russia, as Uriel has been appointed over Russia.

Raphael – His name means "God has healed," and he is over the spirits of men. Some have seen him as the healing angel or over the angels who bring healing.

Raguel – His name means "Friend of God," and he takes vengeance on the world of the luminaries (refers to stars of the heavens, which can also mean angels). Enoch records one of his encounters with Raguel:

From thence I went to another place to the west of the ends of the earth. And I saw a burning fire which ran without resting, and paused not from its course day or night but regularly. And I asked saying: "What is this which rests not?" Then Raguel, one of the holy angels who was with me, answered me and said unto me: "This course of fire which thou hast seen is the fire in the west which persecutes all the luminaries of heaven." (1:7:28-30)

Raguel is the one showing Enoch what vengeance on the luminaries looks like, according to his role as the one who takes vengeance on them.

Michael – His name means "Like God," and he is over the best of mankind and over chaos. Michael has been seen as the chief prince over Israel as well. We also know that Michael is the angel over the apostles, but this is not something Enoch apparently knew.

Saraqael – His name means "Command of God," and he is over the spirits who sin in the spirit.

Gabriel – His name means "Strongman of God," and he is over Paradise, the serpents, and the Cherubim. We also know he is over the prophets and is a messenger of God, like prophets are, but it is not evident that Enoch knew this. One of Enoch's many records of Gabriel reads:

And to Gabriel said the Lord, "Proceed against the bastards and the reprobates, and against the children of fornication and destroy the children of the Watchers from amongst men. Send them one against the other that they

**may destroy each other in battle, for length of days shall
they not have. And no request that they make of thee shall
be granted unto their fathers on their behalf; for they hope
to live an eternal life, and that each one of them will live
five hundred years." (1:4:12)**

We can see here that Gabriel is a strongman of God and does
have authority over the serpents, or those working in
conjunction with Satan, as he was the one sent to destroy those
who were destroying men.

Remiel – His name means "Mercy of God," and he is over
those who rise.

Four of the angels mentioned above seem to be the angels that
Enoch had the most encounters with. They are Michael, Uriel,
Raphael, and Gabriel. One of the things these angels do is
intercede for mankind.

**And then Michael, Uriel, Raphael, and Gabriel looked
down from heaven and saw much blood being shed upon
the earth, and all lawlessness being wrought upon the
earth. And they said one to another, "The earth made
without inhabitant cries the voice of their cryingst up to
the gates of heaven." And now to you, the holy ones of
heaven, the souls of men make their suit, saying, "Bring
our cause before the Most High." And they said to the
Lord of the ages, "Lord of lords, God of gods, King of
kings, and God of the ages, the throne of Thy glory
standeth unto all the generations of the ages, and Thy
name holy and glorious and blessed unto all the ages! Thou
hast made all things, and power over all things hast Thou,
and all things are naked and open in Thy sight, and Thou
seest all things, and nothing can hide itself from Thee.**

Thou seest what Azazel hath done, who hath taught all unrighteousness on earth and revealed the eternal secrets which were in heaven, which men were striving to learn; and Samlazaz, to whom Thou hast given authority to bear rule over his associates. And they have gone to the daughters of men upon the earth, and have slept with the women, and have defiled themselves, and revealed to them all kinds of sins. And the women have borne giants, and the whole earth has thereby been filled with blood and unrighteousness. And now, behold, the souls of those who have died are crying out making their suit to the gates of heaven, and their lamentations have ascended and cannot cease because of the lawless deeds which are wrought on the earth. And Thou knowest all things before they come to pass, and Thou seest these things and Thou dost suffer them, and Thou dost not say to us what we are to do to them in regard to these." (1:4:1-8)

As depicted in this record, angels obviously desire to help the righteous, which is also recorded in the Bible. In Hebrews, angels are described as those who are sent to minister to those who will inherit salvation (Hebrews 1:14).

In response to the angels' request of the Lord, He sends Uriel to Noah to tell him what to do because the flood was coming. He sends Raphael to heal the earth and to bind Azazel (one of the fallen Watcher angels) for his sins in teaching mankind evil. Gabriel is sent to incite the giants to kill each other, and Michael is sent to bind the angel Samlazaz and the other fallen angels who defiled themselves with women.

In another part of the Book of Enoch, it is recorded that four angels stood before the "Lord of glory" praising Him in the following ways:

Michael blessed the Lord of Spirits forever. Raphael blessed Jesus and those who are in Christ. Gabriel prayed and interceded for those who dwell on the earth. And Phanuel fended off the Satans, forbidding them to come before the Lord to accuse those on the earth. The Satans would be evil spirits. (We will expound on that topic later.)

We can learn from these portions of the Book of Enoch that angels help mankind, most especially those who will inherit salvation. They are very strong, and they desire to do the will of the Lord. They also worship God and bring Him praise.

Angels can also take people to heaven. One of the times Enoch was taken to heaven, He saw God on His throne. Enoch recorded the following:

None of the angels could enter and could behold His face by reason of the magnificence and glory and no flesh could behold him. The flaming fire was round about Him, and a great fire stood before Him, and none around could draw nigh Him; ten thousand times ten thousand were before Him, yet He needed no counselor. And the most holy ones who were nigh to Him did not leave by night or depart from Him. (1:5:19-21)

Enoch frequently refers to the angels as holy ones or most holy ones. There are so many of them that Enoch describes them as ten thousand times ten thousand, which would be a hundred million. This is not an exact number, but shows just how great a number of angels the Lord has ministering before Him. It's astonishing!

Enoch also refers to angels as flames of fire. He says, **"Angels took and brought me to a place in which those who were**

61

there were like flaming fire, and when they wished, they appeared as men" (1:6:1). Psalm 104:4 and Hebrews 1:7 also describe angels as flames of fire. And the fact that angels can appear as men is indisputable. Abraham entertained angels who appeared as men in Genesis 18, and Junia tells her audience not to forget to entertain strangers because they might actually be entertaining angels (Hebrews 13:2). Personally, Kirk and I have encountered several angels that we know about who looked like men. And in a vision Kirk saw angels appearing as humans all over the earth. He records:

Jesus turned to me and said, "Come." In a second we were standing in second heaven. Up high, but below the clouds. He pointed down and said, "Look." So I did. There were angels everywhere, and I didn't see any people at all. They were all hidden. He wanted me to see the angels as they did their jobs. Mostly, they looked like regular people! All I could think about was how many of them we must meet each day! Amazing!

Then Jesus said, "Yes, the angels partner with you to work against the demonic. That partnership is complex, but the angels know exactly what they should or shouldn't do. They are also empowered by faith, prayer, and the boldness of the one they are helping. So, have faith! Never cease in prayer! And go in all boldness!" ("Visit to the War Room" – July 21, 2022, *The World and Church Prophecies:* https://a.co/d/6l7Q1jW)

Enoch also records that God renders punishment at the hands of His angels (2:2:66) and that the people (depicted as stars and lightnings) have various numbers of angels working with them (2:1:49-50).

Obviously if we want to understand how to work with angels, it helps to know who they are and what they do. The Book of Enoch can help us with this, but in all things, we should consult the Holy Spirit. He's the Spirit of Truth who leads us into all truth.

Now we'll move on to what Enoch can tell us about the angels who fell from heaven in the days before the flood. We refer to these as Watcher angels. Enoch considered all angels Watcher angels because they watch over mankind, but there are many different kinds of angels. When we refer to Watcher angels, we are referring to the kind that fell by breeding with women.

In the Book of Enoch, we find out what Moses was referring to in Genesis 6 when he writes about the sons of God coming down and procreating with the daughters of men. Jesus, Peter, and Jude also refer to these angels described in the Book of Enoch (Matthew 22:30, 25:41, 2 Peter 2:4, Jude 6). Enoch writes,

And it came to pass when the children of men had multiplied that in those days were born unto them beautiful and comely daughters. And the angels, the children of the heaven, saw and lusted after them, and said to one another: "Come, let us choose us wives from among the children of men and beget us children." (1:3:1-2)

Of the angels who were sent to instruct the children of men to act righteously on the earth, 200 of these angels fell. Their leader, Samlazaz, got them to swear an oath to each other that they would all take wives for themselves and not abandon their plan to leave their place in heaven in order to procreate on the earth. This they did, but they didn't stop there.

The fallen Watcher angels also taught mankind charms, enchantments, and various forms of witchcraft using roots, plants, astrology, etc. They also taught mankind warfare, how to make weapons, and various forms of metal working for the purpose of destruction and not righteousness, among other things (1:3:7-14).

Knowing they had done evil, the Watchers petitioned Enoch to talk to God on their behalf, asking Him to allow them access into heaven and that their children should be saved. God sent Enoch a dream with a scathing rebuke and fierce judgment against the Watchers, the women who sinned with them, and their sons. When Paul says that we shall judge angels, he is no doubt remembering the judgment Enoch brought to the Watchers (1 Corinthians 6:3).

Enoch told the angels their petition for salvation for them and their sons would not be granted, but that they would see the destruction of their sons and then be bound in hell until the lake of fire, and they would have no peace.

The Book of Enoch records the LORD's word to Enoch regarding the fallen Watcher angels:

"... say to the Watchers of heaven, who have sent thee to intercede for them: 'You should intercede for men, and not men for you. Wherefore have ye left the high, holy, and eternal heaven, and lain with women, and defiled yourselves with the daughters of men and taken to yourselves wives, and done like the children of men, have lusted after flesh and blood as those also do who die and perish ... You have no peace." (1:5:24-25, 34)

The sentence that says, "no peace" means these angels are condemned to eternity in hell and the Lake of Fire, condemned to see the destruction of their giant sons, and condemned to know that the destructive so-called mysteries they taught mankind were **"worthless ones"** (1:5:33).

Enoch was then shown a vision of hell in which there was fire, no earth, no heaven, and no water. It was a **"waste and horrible place"** (1:6:17-20). Enoch was told by the angel Uriel regarding the fallen Watchers:

"Here shall stand the angels who have connected themselves with women, and their spirits assuming many different forms are defiling mankind and shall lead them astray into sacrificing to demons as gods. Here they shall stand, till the day of the great judgement in which they shall be judged till they are made an end of." (1:6:22-23)

Contrary to modern so-called science based on evolution, man did not descend from apes, and then mysteriously grow in intelligence over millions of years. Instead, man and woman were very intelligent when they were created on Day 6. Over time, mankind had been desiring to know how things work and how different elements react together (1:4:5) and much more. According to the Book of Enoch, the fallen Watcher angels taught men and women evil "secrets" that men had been desiring to learn. It is written about the fallen Watcher angels,

And they taught them charms and enchantments, and the cutting of roots, and made them acquainted with plants ... And Azazel taught men to make swords, and knives, and shields, and breastplates, and made known to them the metals of the earth and the art of working them, and

bracelets, and ornaments, and the use of antimony, and the beautifying of the eyelids, and all kinds of costly stones, and all colouring tinctures ... And there arose much godlessness, and they committed fornication, and they were led astray, and became corrupt in all their ways. Semjaza taught enchantments and root−cuttings, Armaros the resolving of enchantments, Baraqijal taught astrology, Kokabel the constellations, Ezeqeel the knowledge of the clouds, Araqiel the signs of the earth, Shamsiel the signs of the sun, and Sariel the course of the moon. And as men perished, they cried, and their cry went up to heaven. (1:3:8, 11-14)

To put this in modern language, the angels taught mankind metal working, witchcraft, astrology, and various other occult practices and technologies. They also taught these things to their sons, the giants. Witchcraft, war, and death were the result of these teachings. The Lord said to the Watchers:

"You have been in heaven, but all the mysteries had not yet been revealed to you, and you knew worthless ones, and these in the hardness of your hearts you have made known to the women, and through these mysteries women and men work much evil on earth." (1:5:33)

God has put various elements in the earth and various lights and objects in the heavens to be a blessing to us. But through their corrupt and evil ways, the Watchers taught mankind how to use these very things for evil purposes. Yet, God in his great wisdom and foresight, did not reveal to the Watchers anything of importance. What they knew was "worthless"! Wow!

Think about that. This means what the enemy is doing through the occult, witchcraft, wars, technology, etc. is all worthless.

It's nothing compared to the deep things of God, which are only known through His Spirit. It's no wonder the Lord told us not to pay attention to what the devil was doing during God's Great Reset because it is "irrelevant" (*The World and Church Prophecies: God's Great Reset,* "Angels Going to Battle & What the Devil does is Irrelevant" – June 15, 2020).

What God is doing is what is relevant, and what He is doing is separating the wheat from the tares. He's removing the tares and bringing the earth into a time of tremendous blessing where His Spirit will be poured out in a measure never before seen, where the righteous will move into the places of influence in the world and establish the kingdom of heaven on earth, where Jesus is lifted high, and where the church walks in the authority and power Jesus paid for. Praise God!

Because of the destruction wrought upon the earth due to the actions of the fallen Watcher angels, the Lord sent a deluge to cleanse the earth. We call this Noah's flood. When Moses records that Noah was righteous in his generations, he is referring to not just Noah's righteous heart, but also Noah's bloodline being pure from contamination by the Watcher angels. Just as Peter wrote, "**... the Lord knows how to deliver the godly out of temptations and to reserve the unjust under punishment for the day of judgment...**" (2 Peter 2:9).

Jude and Peter confirmed what Enoch wrote about, that is the punishment against the fallen Watcher angels. Jude and Peter make it clear these angels are in chains reserved for the final judgment. For example, Jude writes, "**And the angels who did not keep their proper domain, but left their own abode, He has reserved in everlasting chains under darkness for the judgment of the great day ...**" (v. 6). And Peter writes,

"God did not spare the angels who sinned, but cast them down to hell and delivered them into chains of darkness, to be reserved for judgment ..." (2 Peter 2:4).

Therefore, according to what is written in the Book of Enoch, Peter's second letter, and Jude's epistle, it is clear that the fallen Watcher angels are no longer around. They are bound in chains in darkness waiting for the final judgment. The angels who did not fall are still serving the Lord. We do not need to concern ourselves with the idea that there are still fallen angels wandering around who are going to seduce women to sleep with them. The fallen angels who had the ability to procreate with women have been bound because of what they did. Father does not want any interbreeding because it causes corruption of what He has made good. God gave me (Tiffany) a dream on September 4, 2024 that illustrates what the Lord thinks of angels procreating with mankind.

I dreamed that there was a farmer who was directing teenage girls to have sex with his pigs. It was disgusting and evil, and I said so. I told my daughter she was not allowed around that kind of stuff. That was the end of the dream.

We asked the Holy Spirit if this dream was from Him, and He said yes. When we asked for the interpretation, the Lord brought to our attention all the movies and shows where there are blue alien women who fall in love with human men and have sex with them, marry them, etc. The Lord says, *"There are no other alien planets or species that want to have sex with humans. It's demonic. If you thought of aliens the way you thought of pigs, you'd be disgusted and know that it is demonic."* This too is how He views the angels who had sex with humans in Enoch's day.

God was grieved regarding mankind, and He determined to destroy him from the **"face of the earth, both man and beast, creeping thing and birds of the air ..."** (Genesis 6:7). **"But Noah found favor in the eyes of the LORD"** (Genesis 6:8, NIV). Then the scriptures explain why Noah found favor. Genesis 6:9 says, **"This is the genealogy of Noah. Noah was a just man, perfect in his generations. Noah walked with God."**

Noah was a just man, meaning a man of faith, for without faith it is impossible to please God (Hebrews 11:6). But Noah was also undefiled by the seed of the fallen Watcher angels. He did not have angel blood in his DNA. The phrase "perfect in his generations," could also be translated "whole in his period of time," meaning he was a whole man without DNA from another species in the time that he lived. Noah may not have been the only lineage that was physically uncorrupted, but he also had faith, being a just man.

This brings us to a question that some people have had regarding the devil's role in corrupting human flesh. Some people believe that the enemy tried to corrupt human flesh because he knew that the Son of God would come as a Man. However, this is really giving the devil too much credit.

First of all, the devil is not all-knowing, nor does he know the future. He only reacts to what is happening. For example, he reacted to the angels and wisemen declaring the birth of the Messiah by instigating King Herod to kill all the boys aged two and under according to the words from the men who followed the star from the East. But, as we know, angels appeared to Joseph in various dreams instructing him to take Jesus and Mary and flee to safety. Apparently, the devil did not find Jesus again until the Lord's baptism. Likely, the enemy assumed Jesus was dead after King Herod ordered the killing of all baby boys aged two and under.

The enemy always uses the same tactics to wipe out the deliverers of the Lord. He did it with Moses, he did it with Jesus, and he's done it with the apostles through the "right" to abortion starting in 1973. But it never works, even with abortion. The Lord said the enemy did not get His great deliverers because He doesn't give His deliverers to those you would expect. No one would expect Jesus to be born to a virgin and her betrothed husband, for example.

After attempting to kill Jesus as a baby, the devil does not appear in Jesus' life again until the Father speaks from Heaven and says, **"This is My beloved Son, in whom I am well-pleased"** (Matthew 3:17). The Spirit then leads Jesus into the desert where the devil comes and tempts Him. At this point, the enemy knows the Son of God is on the earth, but he doesn't understand why.

The demons cry out and say things like, "Have you come to torment us before our time? We know who You are! The Son of God!" (Matthew 8:29) They do not understand what He is doing on earth as a Man. Even when Jesus told His disciples what would happen to him, the devil and the other evil spirits did not understand because the things of the Spirit can only be discerned by the Spirit.

As the Apostle Paul wrote,

[W]e speak the wisdom of God in a mystery, the hidden wisdom which God ordained before the ages for our glory, which none of the rulers of this age knew; for had they known, they would not have crucified the Lord of glory ...

But God has revealed them to us through His Spirit. For the Spirit searches all things, yes, the deep things of God. (1 Corinthians 2:7-8, 10)

If the enemy had known that crucifying the Son of Man would be his demise, he never would have done it. He didn't know because the understanding of what would happen could only come by revelation. The enemy does not get revelation from the Holy Spirit. Similarly, the Jewish leaders did not have revelation either. Even though they had the prophetic words, they did not understand them.

Therefore, while the Watcher angels and their sons, the giants, did corrupt humans and animals, it wasn't because the devil knew that Jesus was coming in the flesh and therefore, he was trying to corrupt the flesh before Jesus could come. No. The enemy did not know what would happen. He cannot see into the future; he only reacts to various things, like the anointing of the Holy Spirit on someone, etc.

In the next chapter, we'll delve into the topic of the Nephilim, who are the offspring of the Watcher angels, and the resulting consequences brought about by their existence.

Chapter 7:
Nephilim/Giants

There is much speculation about giants in the world. Though their bones and tools have most certainly been discovered, for some reason these artifacts and discoveries are covered up and even dismissed outright. There is also some information in the Bible regarding the existence of giants. As it says in Genesis:

Now it came to pass, when men began to multiply on the face of the earth, and daughters were born to them that the sons of God saw the daughters of men, that they were beautiful; and they took wives for themselves of all whom they chose. And the LORD said, "My Spirit shall not strive with man forever, for he is indeed flesh; yet his days shall be one hundred and twenty years. There were giants on the earth in those days, and also afterward, when the sons of God came in to the daughters of men and they bore children to them. Those were the mighty men who were of old, men of renown. (Genesis 6:1-4)

The offspring of some of the fallen Watcher angels and women were giants that are also sometimes called "Nephilim." The book of Genesis records that these giants were men of renown. There are some records of giants after the flood contained within the Bible, like Sihon, Og, Goliath and his brothers, and the fact that David and his mighty men were known as giant killers.

The Book of Enoch records more information regarding giants that can help fill in the gaps we have in the Bible. The Book of Enoch states that the women impregnated by the fallen Watcher angels ...

... became pregnant, and they bare great giants, whose height was three thousand ells: Who consumed the acquisitions of men. And when men could no longer sustain them, the giants turned against them and devoured mankind. And they began to sin against birds, and beasts, and reptiles, and fish, and to devour one another's flesh, and drink the blood. Then the earth laid accusation against the lawless ones. (1:3:9-10)

Some believe the height of three thousand ells was a mistranslation, meant to say that the sons of the Nephilim were called Elioud. However, that the giants were enormous is not an understatement. As the Book of Enoch records, the giants ate everything men could bring them, and when the food ran out, the giants ate the men, animals, and each other. Therefore, the Lord spoke to the angel Raphael and said,

"And heal the earth which the angels have corrupted, and proclaim the healing of the earth, that they may heal the plague, and that all the children of men may not perish through all the secret things that the Watchers have disclosed and have taught their sons" (1:4:11).

The healing of the earth happened through the flood as recorded later in the Book of Enoch where the LORD told the angel Uriel:

"Go to Noah and tell him in my name 'Hide thyself!' and reveal to him the end that is approaching, that the whole

earth will be destroyed, and a deluge is about to come upon the whole earth, and will destroy all that is on it. And now instruct him that he may escape and his seed may be preserved for all the generations of the world." (1:4:9)

Before the Lord sent the flood, however, He gave the following instructions to the angel Gabriel:

"Proceed against the bastards and the reprobates, and against the children of fornication and destroy the children of the Watchers from amongst men. Send them one against the other that they may destroy each other in battle, for length of days shall they not have. And no request that they make of thee shall be granted unto their fathers on their behalf; for they hope to live an eternal life, and that each one of them will live five hundred years." (1:4:12)

Through the judgment against the Watchers and their giant offspring, we can see the love of God for mankind. What the giants did was disgusting and totally evil. They were degenerate and unable to be saved. However, because the giants were part human, the Lord was more lenient with their judgment. They were not sent to hell when they died, but instead, their spirits roam the earth until the final judgment. Since the giants were also part angel, God could have given them a harsher sentence, but He didn't. Mankind, however, no matter how far he has fallen can find redemption and forgiveness through the blood of Jesus Christ. How true it is that God so loved the world, that He gave His only Son (John 3:16). Praise God for His precious gift to us!

Knowing that the giants were only given 500 years to live if they were not killed before that and then that their spirits would roam the earth until the day of judgment, sheds some light on why some of the evil spirits would cry out to Jesus and say things like, **"What have we to do with You, Jesus, You Son of God? Have You come here to torment us before the time?"** (Matthew 8:29). The Nephilim understood there would be a time when they would be thrown into the Lake of Fire to be eternally tormented, but they also knew that time was not supposed to occur until the final judgment. It is the judgment Enoch had pronounced over them. So, it was disconcerting to them to see Jesus casting them out of people. They didn't understand why He had come to earth at that time. They had no understanding of God's plans for salvation.

Jesus did not come to throw them into the Lake of Fire before their time, but that doesn't mean the demonic will have the influence in the future that they have had in the past on humanity. The Lord has said that in His Great Reset, it will be like the enemy is bound because all the tares will be removed, and there will be more of the Holy Spirit poured out. Almost everyone will be filled with the Holy Spirit. The people will not be under the influence of the enemy because they will be followers of Jesus. There will not even be sickness like there was before because the people will not believe the enemy's lies. (For more information see *The Revelation of Jesus Christ and the End Times* and *The World and Church Prophecies: God's Great Reset*.)

Let's move on to the physical evidence of giants. Outside of the Bible and the Book of Enoch there are many records of giants. People have unearthed giant remains, even full skeletons for centuries. They've also unearthed giant weapons and armor. Photos are fairly easy to find. There's even a Book of Giants whose remains evidently date back to 3500 B.C. The scraps of this book are in various languages and difficult to piece together to get a great understanding, but it was evidently a book that kept a record of the history of the giants.

Dr. Jay Winter includes in his translation of the Book of Enoch a short summary regarding the evidence of giants. In it, he writes,

These enormous ancient human beings were worshipped throughout various world religions of which tell of many of them slaying dragons. It is important to note that the term "dragon" was replaced by the word "dinosaur" in 1871 by Sir Edward Owen. Hence, any reference in ancient literature to dragons, is a reference to dinosaurs according to the ontology of the word change associations involved.

(We have found reference to this name change from "dragon" to "dinosaur" as early as 1842 by Sir Richard Owen. The point is that the name was changed.)

Evidence of giants can also be found in drawings and etchings found around the world that depict very large men on thrones with smaller people bowing down and worshiping the ones on the thrones. These etchings are not some far-fetched idea ancient people groups came up with out of thin air. The beings depicted on the thrones are the giants. The giants reportedly killed the dragons (dinosaurs) and were worshiped for doing so until they started killing and eating men.

Crete is one of the most famous places where giants lived. It was once known as Gigantis, or "The Land of Giants." The largest bones to have ever been found that we know of were found on the island of Crete. Dr. Jay Winter writes,

During the Cretan war from 205–200 BC a massive giant skeleton was discovered on the island. This giant was

measured at the length of thirty-three cubits, which equates to nearly 42 feet. The Roman Lucius Flaccus was a notable eyewitness to the gigantic bones, and the Greek writer under Roman Emperor Hadrian, Phlegon of Tralles also mentions the discovery of several giant skeletons.

Crete may have been a hotbed for giants, but their remains have been found all over the world. For example, a giant measuring 19'6" was found in 1577 A.D. in Lucerne, Switzerland. A 23' giant's remains were found in France in 1456 A.D. and another one in France in the 1600's measuring 25'6". In the 1800's a 12'2" giant was found buried in Ireland. And there are many more examples than these.

Besides the remains of the giants themselves, there are also curious finds across the world that are best explained by the fact that people were living with giants nearby. For example, in the Grand Canyon there are what are termed "cliff dwellings" in which people went to great lengths to build homes, granaries, and much more in almost inaccessible places way up high. Why would they go to such lengths unless they were trying to protect themselves from something like a giant that would eat them? This isn't just conjecture. The Native Americans from North America have stories about the giants and how their ancestors were forced to kill the giants to stay alive. Some Native Americans even kept pieces of the giants' hair and wove them into their clothing. One woman in particular who lived in the 1800's wore a dress with orange hair from a giant's head woven into her garment as she tells the story of her ancestors killing off the giants in North America. (See her testimony here: https://youtu.be/Em-ciR1ypyM?si=pV-upBSCD8MXwyA7.)

Besides this, people have also come forth with testimonies of giants alive in recent days. In 2002, it is reported that an U.S. Army squad went missing in the deserts of Afghanistan. A special operation task force went to find out what happened to their missing comrades and came upon a large cave. Around the cave they found broken equipment and gear, as well as blood. They were going to search the cave when a 13-foot tall red-headed, double-toothed giant emerged from the cave and attacked them. He speared one soldier, killing him as the others opened fire, shooting him for a reported thirty seconds in the face until he fell over dead. The soldiers then entered the cave and found the remains of human bones. The giant had evidently eaten the missing Army squad after murdering them. When the special ops reported this encounter to their commanders, the giant's body was loaded into a helicopter and transferred to the United States for "study." Interestingly, there is very limited reporting on this incredible confrontation and evidently the government has nothing more to say on the matter.

Also, there has been a giant caught on camera in the deserts of Portugal in recent years, and there is a four-foot footprint embedded in a rock in South Africa. Even Abraham Lincoln talked about the giants in North America. When he visited Niagara Falls, he said the following:

"When Columbus first sought this continent, when Christ suffered on the cross, when Moses led Israel through the Red Sea, nay, even when Adam first came from the hand of his Maker then as now, Niagara was roaring here. The eyes of that species of extinct giants, whose bones fill the mounds of America, have gazed on Niagara, as ours do now." (universeinsideyou – YouTube)

It was understood in Lincoln's day that the so-called Native American burial mounds were not actually built by the Native Americans. They were built by the giants.

There are many, many more accounts of giants, and we will touch on some of them in the next chapter. For now, we just need to know that the evidence of giants is clear throughout history up to the present time. Why the evidence has been suppressed is another matter that can be explained by how the history of giants proves the existence of God and the truth found in scriptures that give account regarding it.

The book of Genesis starts out, **"In the beginning God created the heavens and the earth"** (Genesis 1:1). Romans 12:20 reads, **"For since the creation of the world His invisible attributes are clearly seen, being understood by the things that are made, even His eternal power and Godhead, so that they are without excuse ..."**. Do you see any issues in these two verses for those of the world system?

The globalists, elitists, cabal, world system adherents, etc. must get God out of the picture if they want the world to follow the system of the world, or the way of the devil, instead of the way of God because God can be seen even in what He has created. Therefore, starting at the beginning of creation, they must remove God. To accomplish this task, they come up with faulty ways of measuring time like carbon dating. They also infiltrate the education system and propagate a theory of billions of years based on evolution. This is all to destroy the truth that in the beginning God created the heavens and the earth.

In fact, it's to destroy the truth that in the beginning, God. God is a problem for the world system adherents. They cannot allow people to believe in God. Therefore, anything that proves there is a God must be eradicated. This is why you can go to national parks like the Grand Canyon where the evidence of enormous amounts of rapidly receding floodwaters is evident in the structure of the canyon, the rock formations and types of rocks, and the abundant fossils of marine life imbedded in the rocks, but the signage will tell you that what your eyes see is not true. You're not allowed to believe in a global flood because if Noah's flood is real, God is real. Instead, you are told what you are seeing happened over hundreds of millions of years, which is simply impossible. But if people are told a lie often enough and especially when the lie is told by so-called experts, they begin to believe it.

Adherents to the world system cannot allow anything that points to God to remain. Therefore, everything they teach is based on evolution over millions or even billions of years. Evolution is a process of the strongest and biggest winning. Enter in the problem of the giants. If evolution is real, why would humans be alive and well and the giants are all buried and gone? If people had evolved into giants, then giants would be here today and not humans. But people didn't evolve into giants. Giants were a mixed breed of angels and humans. The world system cannot tolerate this truth. Therefore, they must get rid of it.

They do this by denying the existence of giants. When you go to national museums, do you see giant remains? Of course not. Museums who used to own the remains of giants and their weapons, armor, and tools have either "lost" them or sold them to people or organizations who are not enlightening the world as to what they have acquired.

We will find in God's Great Reset that these things long hidden from the people of the world will be brought to light. The Lord Jesus said, **"For nothing is secret that will not be revealed, nor anything hidden that will not be known and come to light"** (Luke 8:17). Everything is being exposed. Everything. This is only the beginning. The enemy and those who follow him thought that they could hide the truth, but the truth will come to the light and justice will prevail. And as the Lord said in a prophetic word, *"History books shall be re-written and truth shall be told to those who desire to learn"* (*The World and Church Prophecies: God's Great Reset,* "The Coming In and the Going Out" – February 2, 2022).

It will be shown as history books are re-written, that the giants posed a great problem on the earth. They were great warriors simply because they were so much bigger than everyone else, not to mention they were fathered by angels which gave them a type of supernatural strength, etc. They also had a violent demeanor as evidenced by the fact that in the biblical scriptures they are always depicted as fighters and in the Enochian scriptures we are told they killed men, animals, each other, and they drank blood.

The giants were also ugly. It was not uncommon for them to have extra fingers and toes as evidenced in scripture and in giant remains unearthed over the years (2 Samuel 21:20). Their remains also show they often had more than one row of teeth, just as sharks do. Sometimes they were found with strange protrusions from their ears as well. When we spoke to the Lord about this, asking Him what He considers a giant, He said what He considers giants are grotesque. He doesn't consider a giant someone who is extra tall in today's world. He says the giants were grotesque.

Grotesque means "Characterized by ludicrous, repulsive, or incongruous distortion, as of appearance or manner (synonym: ugly); outlandish or bizarre, as in character or appearance" (The American Heritage® Dictionary of the English Language, 5th Edition). These repulsive creatures were not fully human. They were monsters. Is it any wonder then that the entire Israelite army shook in fear every time Goliath (one of the sons of a giant) came out and called for a man to fight with him?

Contrast what the giants looked and acted like with David. The Lord describes David as ruddy and good-looking, a man after His own heart. David's looks and actions were totally contrary to the looks and actions of the giants. He and his men became known as giant killers because they helped to eradicate their part of the earth of these grotesque monsters.

When God told Adam and Eve to fill the earth and subdue it (Genesis 1:28), they had no idea at the time that their lineage would need to kill angel-human hybrids. But having dominion over the earth means that what is meant to destroy and kill the goodness God created must be extinguished. God gave the earth to men and women, not giants or fallen angels. He raised David and His men up to help eradicate the giant population on the earth so that they would no longer procreate and defile the seed of mankind, not to mention the other horrible things they did.

Though David and his men were much smaller than the monster warriors they fought, they were victorious because the Lord was on their side. As David told Goliath,

"You come to me with a sword, with a spear, and with a javelin. But I come to you in the name of the LORD of

hosts, the God of the armies of Israel, whom you have defied. This day the LORD will deliver you into my hand, and I will strike you and take your head from you. And this day I will give the carcasses of the camp of the Philistines to the birds of the air and the wild beasts of the earth, that all the earth may know that there is a God in Israel. Then all this assembly shall know that the LORD does not save with sword and spear; for the battle is the LORD's, and He will give you into our hands." (1 Samuel 17:45-47)

Of course, David went on to kill Goliath, and the men who followed him later in his life killed the other giants in the area.

In fact, long before David, the Israelites fought giants in the promised land. The Prophet Amos records the Lord speaking of giants in Canaan:

"Yet it was I who destroyed the Amorite before them,
Whose height was like the height of the cedars,
And he was as strong as the oaks;
Yet I destroyed his fruit above
And his roots beneath." (Amos 2:9)

These giants were exactly what the ten spies who brought back a bad report were afraid of. Though Caleb refuted the bad report, the ten spies persisted, saying:

"The land through which we have gone as spies is a land that devours its inhabitants, and all the people whom we saw in it are men of great stature. There we saw the giants (the descendants of Anak came from the giants); and we were like grasshoppers in our own sight, and so we were in their sight." (Numbers 13:32b-33)

Though this was an evil report because it was fear-based instead of faith-based, the spies were right in a factual sense. The giants were known to devour people, and they were of great stature.

But, if Noah's flood wiped out all mankind except those on the ark, where did the giants after the flood come from? Genesis 6:4 reads, **"There were giants on the earth in those days, and also afterward ..."**. This verse has confused many people. If Noah and his family were the only people saved out of the flood, how could there be giants on the earth after the flood? Some think the angels kept procreating with women and made more giants. This is not true. Enoch makes it clear that the fallen Watcher angels were chained before the flood.

And the Lord said unto Michael, **"Go, bind Samlazaz and his associates who have united themselves with women so as to have defiled themselves with them in all their uncleanness"** (1:4:13a).

The fallen Watcher angels were bound in hell, where everyone who is not in Christ goes, until the final judgment at which time they will be sent to the Lake of Fire. Peter and Jude also testify that these angels were bound in hell in chains of darkness (2 Peter 2:4, Jude 6). Since the Watcher angels were bound in hell before the flood, it means some of the giants survived the flood.

The Lord says that the reason some of the giants were able to survive the flood is because of their almost god-like qualities. Being part angel, they had some supernatural-like abilities. Hence swimming for days on end, or clinging to debris for extended periods of time to survive, going without food for long periods of time, etc. The violent waters of the flood over the whole earth scattered these surviving giants over the earth, which is why some were found in North America, some found in Israel, etc. Accounts of the strength of these giants was even being recorded as recently as 1899 in the South Polar Regions, where Dr. Frederick A. Cook observed giant men racing across the land at a rate of 50 miles every few hours (*On the Trail of the Nephilim, Vol. 1* by L.A. Marzulli, p. 32).

However, not many giants survived the flood, and after the flood, they were mainly on the run and in hiding. Their sentence had been passed down to them that they would only live 500 years if they made it that long, and then their life was over. There was no hope for eternity. While they would not be sent to hell, they also could not get to heaven, and so were left to roam the earth as evil spirits until the last judgment when they will be cast into the Lake of Fire (1:4:12, 1:5:28-29).

That the surviving giants procreated is obvious or they would not have been around in David's time, nor currently, if there are any. When we asked the Lord about whether or not the giants had offspring, He said that He's merciful even where no mercy is deserved. It's who He is. But the Lord also said, *"The giants toned down their act because they realized I could move against them and wipe them out anytime I wanted to."*

Basically, the giants started acting in a mode of self-preservation after the flood, for the most part, though not all did this. This would explain the underground cities that have been found and the reported sightings of giants in extreme areas like Antarctica and various deserts. They were (and perhaps are) trying to hide.

Even though they toned down their act for the most part, we can still see the giants wreaking havoc throughout the Old Testament. L.A. Marzulli writes,

"The Nephilim in Canaan were descended from Anak, and so were also known as the Anakim. The Anakim as well as the Emim, Rephaim, and Zanzummim were all a race of giants existing in Canaan at the time of Israel's arrival. Among them were warriors of exceeding stature, including Ishbi-Benob (II Samuel 21:16); Og (Numbers 21:33, Deuteronomony 3:11); and the famous ten-foot-plus Goliath ..." (*On the Trail of the Nephilim, Vol. 1*, p. 129)

Deuteronomy 9:1-3 records,

Hear, O Israel: You are to cross over the Jordan today, and go in to dispossess nations greater and mightier than yourself, cities great and fortified up to heaven, a people great and tall, the descendants of the Anakim, whom you know, and of whom you heard it said, 'Who can stand before the descendants of Anak?' Therefore understand today that the Lord your God is He who goes over before you as a consuming fire. He will destroy them and bring them down before you; so you shall drive them out and destroy them quickly, as the Lord has said to you.

After Israel defeated the giants in the land of Canaan, **"the land had rest from war"** (Joshua 14:15).

Of course, we see there were still some giants among the Philistines in David's day and spread across the world in other places. Most of the giants that did remain were eventually killed by those they tormented, or they simply died off. As mentioned previously, there are accounts of people groups throughout the earth who rose up and killed off giants in their area. But can you see why the Lord has prophesied that even Noah will marvel at God's Great Reset? Because even in Noah's day all the evil wasn't removed. (See *The World and Church Prophecies: God's Great Reset,* "Dare to Dream (With God)" – March 24, 2023.) Any giants still alive today will die naturally or be killed.

The Lord said that He has given the earth to men, not to giants or fallen angels or anyone else, but to men (and women). He wants us to know He knows how to take care of giants, and He knows how to take care of the Cabal (giants of a different kind). All it takes is faith and a slingshot. (Laugh, that was humor!) Back to the Book of Enoch...

Most of our understanding of the Watcher angels and their offspring comes from the Book of Enoch. While Moses mentions them briefly in Genesis 6 and Numbers 13, the giants, otherwise known as Nephilim, are explained more thoroughly in Enoch's writings.

We can trust what Enoch wrote about these Nephilim because it is the same book that Jesus referred to when He told the Sadducees that they didn't know the power of God nor the scriptures (Matthew 22:29-20). When Jesus said they didn't know the scriptures, He was calling Enoch's writings scripture. Therefore, it's just as trustworthy as any other scripture.

Now, let's go back to what happens to the giants when they die. We've discussed that the Watcher angels asked Enoch to intercede for them before God for the spirits of their sons, the giants. They knew they were condemned, but they wanted the Lord to have mercy on their offspring and give them eternal life. However, the Lord condemned the giants by saying through Enoch:

And now, the giants, who are produced from the spirits and flesh, shall be called evil spirits upon the earth, and on the earth shall be their dwelling. Evil spirits have proceeded from their bodies; because they are born from men and from the Watchers is their beginning and primal origin; they shall be evil spirits on earth, and evil spirits shall they be called. And the spirits of the giants afflict, oppress, destroy, attack, do battle, and work destruction on the earth, and cause trouble. They take no food, but nevertheless hunger and thirst, and cause offences. (1:5:28-30)

So, we can see that when a giant dies, its spirit remains on earth until the final judgment. Is there, then, a difference between the spirits who fell with Satan and the spirits of the giants?

In the biblical accounts of Jesus and His disciples casting spirits out of people, the words "demon," "unclean spirit," and "evil spirit" are used interchangeably. One example of this is in the passage where Jesus cast demons out of Mary called Magdelene. The words "demons" and "evil spirits" are used interchangeably.

[A]nd certain women who had been healed of evil spirits and infirmities – Mary called Magdalene, out of whom had come seven demons... (Luke 8:2).

The interchanging of the terms "evil spirits," "demons," and "unclean spirits," is because they're all malevolent spirits who are subject to Satan, and their destination is the Lake of Fire.

All those who sin are subject to Satan. This includes mankind, angels, and hybrids. We're either slaves of sin or slaves of righteousness (Romans 6:18). As Jesus told the Jews, their father was the devil (John 8:44). Only those who are born again into Christ, who put their faith in Jesus, shall be saved. The rest are of the devil. As those who cannot be saved, the spirits of the giants are under the authority of the devil.

When the Lord cursed the serpent in the Garden of Eden, He said that the seed of the serpent and the seed of the woman would be at enmity with each other (Genesis 3:15). The seed of the devil can be understood as people who follow Satan (Jesus called the Jews "sons of the devil" in John 8:44), but the seed could also be considered the Nephilim, as they are under the jurisdiction of Satan.

Satan himself is not capable of procreating. If he could, he wouldn't go to all this trouble of genetic engineering, etc. to corrupt the human race. He'd just do it himself. But he can't; he's a spirit. The Watcher angels were a different type of angel. They were capable of procreating, but the Lord took away their ability by reserving them in chains for judgment because they misused what they had been given.

We do not need to concern ourselves too much with what Satan and those under his authority are doing. We just need to set our sights on them and pull the trigger. Our job is to bring the kingdom of Heaven to earth. We cast out the demonic, and we bring the rule and reign of Jesus Christ through His Holy Spirit everywhere we go. He who is in us is greater than he who is in the world; whether that is a fallen angel or the offspring of a fallen angel because Jesus is always greater. Amen.

Chapter 8:
Mysteries of Enoch

———————◆O◆———————

Likely to be the longest chapter of the book, the "Mysteries of Enoch" are mysteries that are brought to the light to prepare us for the truth.

As mentioned in the last chapter, giants appeared after the flood all over the earth. And yet the records and evidence of giants are mostly hidden. When something that corroborates the evidence of giants is discovered, it disappears and sometimes the person who brought it to light disappears too. Why are the skeletons of giants taken by the Smithsonian and other various government entities never seen again? Why do these types of organizations hide the evidence that dinosaurs (previously always called "dragons") and mammoths were killed by men, proving a co-existence with men? Why is the obvious working of giants in megalithic structures like Stone Henge and the Great Pyramid attributed to other people groups?

Do some of these questions surprise you? Let's delve into some of the mysteries Enoch can help explain.

Giant Remains

We discussed the Nephilim in the last chapter, but we'll explore a little more in this section. Giant remains have been found on every continent on earth with the possible exception of Antarctica. Although as mentioned previously, there are eyewitness reports of live giants on Antarctica as recently as 1899. A newspaper article dated August 5, 1899 from the *Youngston Vindicator*, p. 5, records testimony from Dr. Frederick A. Cook who asserted that he saw "monstrous" men and women who wore furs, and the men were armed with bows, arrows, and clubs, and could outrun any horse on a long stretch (Marzulli, L. A., *On the Trail of the Nephilim*, p. 32). Therefore, while remains have not yet been reported as being found in Antarctica, there are reports of live giants living there in recent times.

This information is incredible, but it also validates what the Holy Spirit said about some of the Nephilim surviving the great deluge in Noah's day. The Holy Spirit also said that after the flood, the giants became more subdued, not that they still weren't evil, but they sometimes went into hiding because they knew their days were numbered. The many cities found underground and in caves give credence to this truth as well.

Some caves have been found containing giant bones, giant tables, giant chairs, giant weapons, etc. And yet museums that sometimes display ax heads or spear tips that are much too large and heavy for a man of normal stature to wield will tell you that what you're looking at was used ceremoniously by regular-sized men. What they neglect to tell you is probably more important than what they do tell you. They neglect to tell you where or by what the ax head or spear tip was found. Was it found beside a giant skeleton? Was it found by a mammoth or dinosaur (dragon)? Why is this type of information kept from the people?

Back to the many finds of giant skeletons. *Scientific American*, p. 106, on August 14, 1880 records the account of a mound opened in Ohio in which were found various skeletons of male and female giants, some as small as eight feet and others as long as ten feet (Marzulli, L. A., *On the Trail of the Nephilim*, p. 21). And in Virginia someone found a tooth measuring 3 inches wide by 5 inches long. In comparison, the average adult front tooth is only 6-7 millimeters in width. Where did this tooth come from?

Sometimes we talk about how tall the giants are, but they were proportioned in a way that made them big all around. For example, a nine-foot skeleton of a man that was found had a two-foot-deep chest cavity. That's really large!

Many of the skeletal remains of giants are found in giant burial mounds. We've been told these mounds are Native American burial mounds, and therefore, we're not allowed to disturb them. However, newspaper articles abound in the 1800's and early 1900's of people digging up these mounds and finding giant bones. These sorts of discoveries are recorded across the globe. In France in the 1500's and 1600's for example there were found skeletons up to 25 ft and more! These discoveries were made public at the time, but now we're not allowed to know about them.

Every culture and religion tells of giants in their history. The scriptures contained in the Bible tell of giants, as well. For example, Nimrod who ruled over Babel and oversaw the building of the tower of Babel, which is believed to have been some sort of portal, was a giant. But outside the Bible there are many accounts as well. The well-known story of Gilgamesh in Sumerian history is all about a giant who ruled for over 100 years. Then there's the story of Paul Bunyon who was a giant lumberjack. And of course, all the mythological stories of demi-gods, which were half gods and half humans. The offspring of an angel and a human would fit this category.

Perhaps the fables, tall tales, and mythologies are based in reality after all.

The evidence of giants is all around us. As an example, the Native Americans say that their ancestors killed the giants who were in North America. For instance, the Mohawk and Huron tribes relate that they banded together, attacked, and killed all the giants in their lands who had been killing and eating their people. These giants were known as the Allegeni giants, and the Allegheny Mountain Range still bears the name of this particular tribe of giants that the Mohawks and Hurons wiped out. (See *On the Trail of the Nephilim II* by L. A. Marzulli, p. 33.)

There is also evidence right before our eyes in many of the so-called mountains of the earth. Using a trusted search engine, you can search for mountains that look like giants. You will see what looks like many giants who have been petrified, perhaps by volcanic ash when the ground broke up before and during the beginning of Noah's flood. There are also petrified tree stumps that we are told are mountains and even petrified enormous animals, like elephants and snakes. We know there were giant men, but if these so-called mountains are indeed giant animals and trees, where did they come from?

When Enoch wrote that the Watchers taught their sons and the humans secret knowledge and that the giants sinned against animals, was he referencing manipulating creation to make giant animals and plants that could sustain giants? After all, these giants ate everything men brought them. They needed something more to sustain themselves. Is this also where dinosaurs (dragons) came from? This theory makes more sense than believing God created the T-Rex or the velociraptor. It also makes sense that God would save intact humans and

93

animals on the ark and wipe out the altered creations brought about by the Watchers and their sons. It even explains what the deep state, cabal, and Luciferians are doing and trying to do with CERN. They communicate with these evil spirits from the past to gain knowledge so they can more effectively work evil today. Some of these people even believe they come from the bloodlines of the Watcher angels.

Whether they do or not is irrelevant. These are nothing compared to the blood of Jesus. The Lord says, "The flesh profits nothing." He's not concerned with what's in their bloodlines. It's agreement with the demonic that matters, and these globalists agree with the devil. It's no wonder we need a reset, and that God says even Noah will be impressed with what God does in our day!

Technology, Knowledge, and Megalithic Structures

Enoch writes about the Watcher angels: **"And they taught them charms and enchantments, and the cutting of roots, and made them acquainted with plants"** (1:3:8). What the Watchers taught their sons and taught mankind was evil. We discussed it briefly in the last section, but additionally, consider drugs like hallucinogens for example. We know that shamans and other "wise men" have used hallucinogens for centuries to more easily allow interaction with demons. Well, it was the Watchers who released this knowledge and other previously unknown knowledge on the earth.

For example, accounts of relics made of metal and rock that belies the understanding abound. There have been metal relics found of a substance that not only does not break easily, but does not scratch when assaulted. This is foreign to our current knowledge of metal working.

There have been found artwork of flying men on textiles in Paracas, Peru. According to oral history passed down to the Paracas people, these drawings are depictions of flying men who came from the sky and taught the men of Earth special knowledge. This sounds a lot like what Enoch wrote:

And Azazel taught men to make swords, and knives, and shields, and breastplates, and made known to them the metals of the earth and the art of working them, and bracelets, and ornaments, and the use of antimony, and the beautifying of the eyelids, and all kinds of costly stones, and all colouring tinctures ... Semjaza taught enchantments and root–cuttings, Armaros the resolving of enchantments, Baraqijal taught astrology, Kokabel the constellations, Ezeqeel the knowledge of the clouds, Araqiel the signs of the earth, Shamsiel the signs of the sun, and Sariel the course of the moon. (1:3:11-13)

One Native American from the Taino tribe testifies that the Indians did not build the Great Circle Mound or the Octagonal Mound in Ohio, as we're told. Instead, he says that the giants built these mounds while overseen by the "Star People," which would be the Watcher angels. "This is why these complexes are astronomically aligned perfectly according to the timing of different celestial occurrences" (Marzulli, *On the Trail of the Nephilim II*, p. 34).

Recently in Ecuador there has been found an ancient lost city with a giant stone wall surrounding it that contains several pyramids that glow blue at night. What sort of rocks or technology causes the blue color? It's certainly a mystery.

We've been fed the story that the Egyptians built the pyramids with the forced labor of their slaves. However, common sense tells us that the ability to build the Great Pyramid and many other pyramids around the world with the precision, large stones, and knowledge of the sun, moon, and stars, was not only unlikely, but nonsensical. This is besides the fact that the Great pyramid "has eight sides that are only visible by air on the equinoxes, and its mass is related to *pi*" (Sanger, Laura, *The Roots of the Federal Reserve,* p. 64). Why make something with stones that no one can lift, when you can do it with stones that are easily maneuverable? How could something be created by people who supposedly didn't understand *pi* and couldn't fly so wouldn't build something that is only visible from the sky (eight sides)? Stonehenge in England (previously called "The Giants' Ring"), the American Stonehenge, many of the large pyramids, enormous walls, and other gigantic structures were obviously built by giants. Once we understand giants actually lived on earth, everything begins to make more sense.

In fact, in Mexico, there have been found the remains of giants whose clothing had depictions of pyramids on them. The natives who live(d) in Mexico, the United States, and other areas confess(ed) that their ancestors did not build these megalithic structures, but that instead they were built by a giant race of beings who came before them. This is true regarding the "Indian Mounds" as well. Native Americans will often say that these mounds were not built by their people.

Probably the most striking visual that shows giants were the constructors of giant structures around the earth is found in Cusco, Peru. There are structures in Cusco where the bottom layer is built out of enormous stones weighing tons of pounds and quarried from 40-50 miles away. These stones were cut with such precision that no mortar was used between them.

They fit like a glove together. They seem to incorporate some sort of technology that was able to soften the stones in order to cut and shape them easily so they would lock together and harden again. These sorts of building projects have been attributed to the Incas by the historical elite who tell us what to believe about history. However, built on top of these mega structures is a layer of brick work incredibly inferior to the first layer. This was the layer actually built by the Incas. Then on top of that layer can be found a layer of brick work laid by the Spanish, which is better than the Inca's work, but neither holds a candle to the base layer of gigantic stones. Any normal person, who had not been brainwashed by so-called "historical experts" would never believe a normal man could build the buildings and structures found in Peru and around the world that defy modern feats of machinery and technology.

Some of the enormous constructions that defy logic seem to be connected to one another. First of all, there are mega structures made out of piezoelectric rock with trapezoidal "windows" in them. Piezoelectric rock carries a frequency, and it is believed that the trapezoid openings in these structures helped to achieve a certain frequency that could be carried to other giant structures. Some believe that these structures around the world could have been some sort of grid that allowed the Nephilim to communicate with each other either physically and/or spiritually.

For example, American Stonehenge is a direct line to England Stonehenge. There are also connections between pyramids around the world. In fact, the Great Pyramid in Giza may have been a mega hydrogen generator, which technology would be easy today but unexplained according to the history we're taught of when the pyramids were built (Marzulli, *On the Trail of the Nephilim*, p. 219). It would have been very easy to make a grid before the earth was flooded. It could have been done afterwards as well.

This would also explain the deep state's infatuation with pyramids, and it lends credence to the idol worship of the Watchers and Nephilim, as they had technologies and abilities far advanced from humans who had not been taught the same.

Besides the megalithic circular stone structures of American Stonehenge and England Stonehenge, there are other circular structures built around the world that some believe were perhaps a grid for the demonic and/or portals for the demonic to use. A portal is an opening for the angels of God or the demonic to use, depending where it is connected. Let's look at this a little more in-depth.

John 1:51 reads: **He** [Jesus speaking to Nathaniel] **then added, "Very truly I tell you, you will see heaven open, and the angels of God ascending and descending on the Son of Man."** In this passage, Jesus is referencing what we refer to as "Jacob's Ladder." When Jacob was on his way to Haran, he had a dream in which there was a ladder set up on earth, and its top reached heaven. The angels of God were ascending and descending on it. And the LORD was at the top of the ladder, speaking to Jacob (Genesis 28:10-22). In effect, what Jacob was seeing was a portal from earth to heaven. Therefore, Jesus was telling Nathaniel what an open heaven looks like.

The word "upon" in the Greek can mean: "upon, on, at, by, before, of position, over, against, to, and across" (Strong's G1909). In other words, when the portal to heaven is opened, the angels are ascending and descending through that portal all around the person who opened it.

Put in simplistic terms, the heavens are divided into three parts. First heaven is earth. Second heaven is where the angels and demonic do battle. It is above the earth. Third heaven is what we traditionally consider heaven where the saints, angels, and the Lord dwell.

In Christ, we have authority to open and close portals. This means both heavenly and demonic portals. Without a portal opened, the angels must do battle every time they pass through the heavens. With a portal opened, they can bypass the battle and accomplish their tasks much more easily.

Witches and others on the side of the enemy open portals for the demonic. Those portals come up out of the earth. We have authority to close those just as much as we have authority to open heavenly portals.

We are tasked with working with the angels. They are fellow servants with us. The saints on earth and the angels in heaven benefit from open portals connecting heaven to earth. You may want to open a portal above your home, your work, your school, yourself, etc. Use your authority to close the demonic portals and open the heavenly ones wherever the Holy Spirit directs you to do so.

With this in mind, it is possible these circular structures, which generally had a phallic symbol or some sort of point in the middle could be open portals to the demonic. Interestingly, Washington, D.C. and many other important cities in the world have a circular design in them that includes a phallic symbol in the middle of it. Why would our important cities be built with this kind of symbolism? What is the connection to the same sort of structures built by the giants? Are these circular layouts connected spiritually around the world? For what purpose would that be? What should we do about this as those with authority in Christ?

What the giants have built as far as a grid and/or communication system is seemingly complex and deliberate because they needed to be. Our access to heaven is one way. It's Jesus. And yet, we can learn something here about being deliberate in closing portals to hell and opening portals to heaven. We can change the atmosphere in areas by breaking curses and releasing the Holy Spirit and the angels of God.

Big Foot, Dinosaurs, and Aliens

The word "dragon" used to be used instead of the word "dinosaur" to mean the same creatures. The word change came about in 1842. A man named Sir Richard Owen from England named the fossils, many of which were previously considered "dragons," to "Dinosauria," which means "terrible lizard." Because of this change, scientists and historians were able to dismiss dragon legends as myth and declare that dinosaurs lived millions or billions of years ago before man ever evolved from an ape. This ridiculous theory has been promoted as truth to civilization for over a hundred years.

But the theory of evolution cannot explain why a woolly mammoth with fur and meat on it could be found frozen in ice after millions of years. Or how weapons could be found next to dinosaur bones. Or even why a tribe in the Amazon describes a creature that sounds exactly like a brontosaurus, whom they call a "river blocker." There's even a photograph from the civil war that shows civil war soldiers standing around a dead pterodactyl. Now, are these all true stories? Are they all a hoax?

Then, too, what about Big Foot sightings? We are used to believing all these sightings are a ruse. But are they? Couldn't what people describe as sasquatches be actual giants? The following is the definition for "sasquatch" as defined by Brittanica:

"Sasquatch, a large, hairy, humanlike creature believed by some people to exist in the northwestern United States and western Canada. It seems to represent the North American counterpart of the Himalayan region's mythical monster, the Abominable Snowman, or Yeti. The name 'Sasquatch' derives from the Salish word *se'sxac*, which means 'wild men.' The creature is also commonly called Bigfoot."

We know that giants were (are?) ugly. Couldn't some of them possibly be hairy as well?

Then too, there have been supposed alien sightings. Do these have anything to do with giants? Do the orbs of light have to do with the demonic?

If we've learned anything through the COVID scam, it's that we should not believe everything we're told. In fact, we should almost always believe the exact opposite of what the media and the elites tell us because they are trying to hide the truth. They do not want us aware of their evil schemes, the true age of the earth, or the true origin of man. They're Satanists at their core, lying just like their father, the devil.

Strange Customs

Have you ever wondered why certain people groups had strange customs like disfiguring their skulls? The practice of skull shaping is called cradle boarding. There have been numerous elongated giant skulls found in Peru that cannot be attributed to cradle boarding. There has even been a giant baby found in a giant woman's skeleton with an elongated skull, proving some giants were born with these types of skulls. Additionally, these giant skulls do not have the same bone structure as a normal human skull. There have also been found giant skulls in various areas of the world with other deformities.

We know that the Nephilim were worshiped as gods across the earth from various pictographs and pieces of artwork left behind from ancient civilizations. Therefore, when we see people groups cradle boarding their babies in order to shape their heads a certain way, couldn't we surmise these societies were deforming the heads of their children in order to make them look similar to their gods?

Is it any wonder then that God told His people not to alter the shape of their skulls? The Lord says in Leviticus 19:27-28, **"You shall not round off the hairline of your heads, nor trim the edges of your beard."** In the actual Hebrew, this verse says, **"You shall not round the corners of your head or your chin."** The Lord was not concerned with the Israelites' haircuts, but that they were not emulating the "gods" of the people around them.

All of these are interesting mysteries that the Lord will reveal the answers to in time to come. But in the meantime, we should consider why we would want to believe the government and scientists over the Native Americans, Peruvians, Africans, and other people groups who testify to what they have seen and heard. To quote L. A. Marzulli in his book *On the Trail of the Nephilim II*, he says:

"We have account after account after account here in the states of the Smithsonian coming in and taking these bones and they are never seen again. I mean if it were just one or two, I would dismiss it as hearsay. We've literally got scores of eyewitness testimony; doctors, medical people, and scientists from the earlier part of the twentieth century stating that they called the Smithsonian, and they said they would get back to us and we never hear anything about it at all." (p. 96)

It's obvious that we have been lied to about many things. Yet, overcorrection would be just as detrimental. We need the truth, and it is the Spirit of Truth who leads us into all truth. The Lord spoke to Kirk regarding this on July 10, 2024:

"Prophet, your generation has been systematically lied to about many things. Much of what you would consider 'truth' is a lie, or mostly lies. It is not required of you and your Apostle to 'make right' these lies right now. I AM only requiring you to open the eyes of the people so that when the truth is brought forth, then they will recognize it.

There are those whose job and passion will be to unearth the truth. They will be led by My Spirit to use real science and the unbiased knowledge and wisdom that He will bring to this subject. In truth, all of the seven mountains of influence are rotten to the core. History is but one of the areas that needs to be corrected. I AM raising up an army of My Own to bring a massive change to everything you think you 'know.'

Open the hearts and minds of those who desire to know the 'truth.' I AM the Truth! And I will set free those who will come to Me! For now, just know that a time of great change is coming. Allow a time of mystery and of not knowing. For there are those who will be uncovering the lies and spreading the truth by the Spirit of God. Amen." ("People Coming Who Will Unearth the Truth by the Spirit" – July 10, 2024)

The Lord also said in a previous prophecy that history books would be rewritten for those who desired to know the truth. ("The Coming In and the Going Out" – February 1, 2022, *The World and Church Prophecies: God's Great Reset,* https://a.co/d/8vNZOCH) We look forward to that. In the meantime, we are raising questions that open our hearts and minds to be ready to receive the truth.

Chapter 9:
Jesus

All scripture bears witness to Jesus Christ. The writings of Enoch are no exception. References to Jesus abound in the Book of Enoch. He's never called "Jesus," as that is the name given to Him when He came to earth as a Man (none of the prophets in the Old Testament called the Son of God "Jesus" either), but He's called "The Elect One," "The Holy Great One," "Righteous One," and other such names by Enoch. In fact, the Book of Enoch starts out prophesying about Jesus. It reads, **"I saw the vision of the Holy One in the heavens ... The Holy Great One will come forth from His dwelling ... And the eternal God will tread upon the earth"** (1:1:2-4). Enoch is speaking of seeing Jesus in the heavens. He is prophesying that Jesus will come out of Heaven to earth.

As Enoch continues prophesying in this portion of the Book of Enoch, he alludes to Jesus bringing salvation, justice in the days of Noah, and bringing justice in the last days. He uses phrases that are very familiar to those of us who have read the Bible. For example, Enoch prophesies:

But with the righteous He will make peace.
And will protect the elect,
And mercy shall be upon them.
And they shall all belong to God,
And they shall be prospered,
And they shall all be blessed.

And He will help them all,
And light shall appear unto them,
And He will make peace with them. (1:1:8)

After this, Enoch prophesies that there will be forgiveness of sins and salvation for the righteous, but for the sinners **"there shall be no salvation but on** [them] **all shall abide the curse of the beast. But for the elect there shall be light and joy and peace, and they shall inherit the earth"** (1:2:11-14). This is an obvious reference to what the "Holy Great One" was going to do when He came to earth. And as noted before, Jesus is also referred to as "the Elect One." Therefore, Enoch refers to everyone who is in Christ as the "elect" because they are found to be in the Elect One.

Interestingly too, Enoch refers to the works of the elect as works of the Holy Spirit and as works that were chosen for the righteous to do by the Lord. It is written,

And when the Righteous One shall appear before the eyes of the righteous, whose elect works hang upon the Lord of Spirits, and light shall appear to the righteous and elect who dwell on the earth, where then will be the dwelling of the sinners, and where the resting-place of those who have denied the Lord of Spirits? It had been good for them if they had not been born. (2:1:5)

Jesus is the Righteous One in this passage, and the works done by Jesus and by those in Him "hang upon the Lord of Spirits," meaning they are done through the working of the Holy Spirit. Those who deny the Lord have no "resting place" or no peace. In other words, they are not saved. As Jesus says about Judas in Matthew 26:24, **"… woe to that man by whom the Son of Man is betrayed! It would have been good for that man if**

106

he had not been born." Jesus quotes Enoch almost word for word here.

Prophets of the Lord will exalt Jesus because the Holy Spirit is the Spirit of Prophecy, and He testifies of Jesus (John 15:26). Therefore, the Book of Enoch is full of the exaltation of Jesus because Enoch was a prophet. As we noted before, Enoch does not call Jesus by the name Jesus, but has many other names for Him. "Elect One" is one of Enoch's common names for Jesus. For example, when Enoch saw heaven in one of his visions, he saw the angel Raphael blessing **"the Elect One and the elect ones who hang upon the Lord of Spirits"** (2:1:29). This is a direct reference to Jesus and those found in Him who are born of His Spirit.

The portion of the Book of Enoch entitled "The Second Parable" contains the most direct references to Jesus. Enoch says that those who have denied the name of the Lord of Spirits (meaning denied the name of Jesus) shall be judged (2:2:2). And Enoch notes that the righteous will also be judged by the Lord Jesus. He writes,

On that day Mine Elect One shall sit on the throne of glory and shall try their works, and their places of rest shall be innumerable. And their souls shall grow strong within them when they see Mine Elect Ones. And those who have called upon My glorious name: Then I will cause Mine Elect One to dwell among them. (2:2:3-4)

Sounds reminiscent of John 1:14, **"And the Word became flesh and dwelt among us..."**.

Not only is Jesus referred to as the Elect One by whom mankind can be saved, but He's also referred to by Enoch as the Son of Man. Enoch asks the angel who was showing him these things about the Son of Man, and the angel replied:

"This is the Son of Man who hath righteousness. With whom dwelleth righteousness, and who reveals all the treasures of that which is hidden. Because the Lord of Spirits hath chosen him and whose lot hath preeminence before the Lord of Spirits in uprightness for ever." (2:2:9)

Is it any wonder that the religious leaders of Jesus' day were offended when Jesus called Himself the Son of Man? They were well acquainted with the writings of Enoch. They knew what He was saying. The Son of Man was going to come from Heaven because He was the Son of God. So, Jesus was saying He was the Son of God.

Not only that, but Jesus was saying He had preeminence, just as Enoch stated. And Jesus truly is the preeminent One. Whatever we believe about God, we must see in Jesus because Jesus is preeminent in all things. He is the first and the last, the beginning and the end. He is before all things and above all things and all things consist in Him. As Enoch states: **"Yea, before the sun and the signs were created, before the stars of the heaven were made, His name was named before the Lord of Spirits"** (2:2:23).

Then Enoch testifies that the Son of Man **"shall be a staff to the righteous ... the light of the Gentiles, and the hope of those who are troubled in heart"** (2:2:24). All of these references are also found in the Bible. Enoch goes on ... **"All who dwell on the earth shall fall down and worship before Him, and will praise and bless and celebrate with song the Lord of Spirits ... For in his name they are saved ..."** (2:2:25, 27).

These verses from the Book of Enoch are clear references to Jesus and are stated in similar wording in the Bible as well. We're told that every knee will bow, and every tongue confess that Jesus is Lord, and that there is no other name by which we are saved (Philippians 2:10-11, Acts 4:12).

Enoch also testifies that wisdom is found in Christ. He writes, **"And in Him dwells the spirit of wisdom, and the spirit which gives insight, and the spirit of understanding and might, and the spirit of those who have fallen asleep in righteousness"** (2:2:33).

Of course, Paul testifies that all wisdom and knowledge are hidden in Christ in Colossians 2:3 (**"... in whom are hidden all the treasures of wisdom and knowledge"**). And the Prophet Isaiah speaks of the Spirit of Christ in a similar manner to Enoch. He writes regarding Jesus:

There shall come forth a Rod from the stem of Jesse,

And a Branch shall grow out of his roots.

The Spirit of the LORD shall rest upon Him,

The Spirit of wisdom and understanding,

The Spirit of counsel and might,

The Spirit of knowledge and of the fear of the LORD. (Isaiah 11:2)

Jesus is also depicted as the one who judges in the Bible and in the Book of Enoch. Paul writes that **"we must all appear before the judgment seat of Christ"** (2 Corinthians 5:10). And Enoch writes,

And He shall judge the secret things and none shall be able to utter a lying word before Him for He is the Elect One before the Lord of Spirits according to His good pleasure ... And He is righteous also in His judgement and in the presence of His glory unrighteousness also shall not maintain itself: At His judgement the unrepentant shall perish before Him. (2:2:34, 38)

Whether Jesus is referred to as the Elect One, the Righteous One, the Son of Man, a light to the Gentiles, a staff to the righteous, the Holy One, or some other name, it is indisputable that the Book of Enoch exalts Jesus and presents Him as the preeminent One. Jesus is King of kings and Lord of lords. As the angels declared before Him:

"Lord of lords, God of gods, King of kings, and God of the ages, the throne of Thy glory standeth unto all the generations of the ages, and Thy name holy and glorious and blessed unto all the ages! Thou hast made all things, and power over all things hast Thou, and all things are naked and open in Thy sight, and Thou seest all things, and nothing can hide itself from Thee. (1:4:4)

There are many more references to Jesus in the Book of Enoch than what are written here because every true prophet will exalt Jesus. The Spirit of Prophecy is the Holy Spirit. As prophets are led by the Spirit of Christ, they will lift up Jesus. Amen and amen.

Chapter 10:
Importance of Enoch's Writings

E ven though Enoch's son Methuselah preserved Enoch's writings and passed them to Noah, who passed them to Shem, who passed them to Abraham (as the book of Jasher, which is historical but embellished, records), and from there they were passed on to Abraham's descendants, the writings of Enoch were suppressed for centuries and only read by small groups of people until now. This comes as no surprise to the LORD or to Enoch himself, as the Book of Enoch begins with these words:

The words of the blessing of Enoch, wherewith he blessed the elect and righteous, who will be living in the days of tribulation, when all the wicked and godless are to be removed. And Enoch, a righteous man whose eyes were opened by God took up his parable and said, "I saw the vision of the Holy One in the heavens, which the angels showed me, and from them I heard everything, and from them I understood as I saw, but not for this generation, but for a remote one which is for to come." (1:1:1-2)

When the Lord is about to do a thing, He speaks to His friends, the prophets, about such things. As the Prophet Amos has written: **"Surely the Lord GOD does nothing, / Unless He reveals His secrets to His servants the prophets"** (Amos 3:7).

Sometimes what the Lord reveals to His servants, the prophets does not come to pass for a long time. Enoch's prophecies are no exception. When we spoke to the Lord about why He was bringing the Book of Enoch to light right now, He said:

"Enoch is My friend, and he prophesied that his book would come forth in the end times for a distant generation. Prophet, the Book of Enoch was written for your generation. Have you noticed that it confirms everything that I AM telling you to make known? Therefore, Enoch's book has not been necessary in the past, but it is becoming more so with each passing day.

Your generation shall know the Truth, and the Truth shall set you free. Free from the bondage of money or lack of it, free to work WITH heaven (angels), free from the lies that say God is weak and the lies that say His Church is even weaker (and needs to be raptured to save it)!

I AM confirming My true Apostles and Prophets using the writings of Enoch!" Amen.

Besides all of this, the Lord is saying that the revealing of the Book of Enoch also exposes the institutional church because they will not pick it up. They idolize the Bible as the "word" and will not look elsewhere for a word from the Lord.

Whenever a lawyer is making his case before a judge or jury, he brings in witnesses to corroborate his narrative. If he is prosecuting a case, he will bring in testimony after testimony that proves the defendant is guilty. If he is defending a case, he will bring in witness after witness and document after document to prove the innocence of his client. Scripture works similarly to evidence in a courtroom. It proves what God is saying and doing.

When we read the Bible with the Holy Spirit, we will see that it testifies to God's narrative throughout. It testifies to His goodness, His victory over darkness, His love for all creation, that He is the Creator, that though mankind fell, the Son of God has come to redeem us back to God, and much more.

Scripture is also useful as a witness to what the Holy Spirit is currently speaking. Sometimes when we hear God, we're not sure what we've heard is correct, and we need Him to tell us again in a different way. In these cases, we may say something like, "I think I've heard You, but God if this is You, please show me in the scriptures." Then we will listen for Him to tell us to look at something that has been written down as evidence that He's spoken to us. This sort of witness can come in other ways too, of course. Sometimes He will prove what He's said through someone else, an event, a dream, a vision, or any number of ways. But using scripture is one way He confirms or denies what we've heard.

The first half of the Book of Enoch can be considered scripture, and it is therefore a way that the Holy Spirit can use to confirm His words to us, confirm His narrative of justice to us, confirm Jesus is the Christ, confirm God's narrative of victory for the righteous in the end times, and much more.

Often when Jesus taught using parables, He would say something about those with ears to hear and eyes to see. These are the ones who would be given understanding. Ears to hear and eyes to see means that we have been born again of the Spirit of Christ. As Jesus told Nicodemus, **"[U]nless one is born again, he cannot see the kingdom of God"** (John 3:3). Those who are born again are born of the Spirit of Christ (John 3:5). And it is the Spirit of Christ who shows us the mysteries of God (1 Corinthians 2:10-11).

Therefore, it is essential that we have the Spirit of God to understand the things of God. Listening to and following the Holy Spirit is absolutely necessary for a born-again Christian. The way of the Spirit is the Jesus way. Never does Jesus instruct His disciples that they must learn to read. He never says that an education is necessary to become one of His followers. He says we need hearts that are open to Him, hearts with ears attentive to His voice and eyes attentive to what He is doing.

Therefore, it is not absolutely necessary for a born-again Christian to read the Book of Enoch. It is not necessary to know what is in the Book of Enoch. It is not necessary to study it at all. In fact, it is not necessary to read anything. It's necessary to listen to His voice and follow Him.

In following the Spirit of Christ, if He tells you to learn to read, then learn to read. If He tells you to read the Book of Enoch, or the Bible, or some other document, then read it. You get no brownie points for doing anything outside of His Spirit. It's only in following that we receive rewards. So, don't let knowledge and learning usurp following the Spirit of Christ. Jesus said our work was to believe Him (John 6:29). That belief is born out through obedience to what we hear Him say (John 14:15, 1 John 2:3). Obedience to His voice is what is necessary.

That being said, the Book of Enoch is important to understand because it bears witness to what the Lord is speaking to His prophets right now, and it bears witness to what is happening on earth right now. For example, though we do not have physical giants trying to take over mankind, we have another form of giants found in technology, like Artificial Intelligence. But just as the Lord did not allow the fallen angels or their offspring to have dominion in the earth, so He is not going to allow technology in the hands of a few to gain dominion in the earth. The following prophecies are included to encourage your faith and give you a vision of what God's plans are regarding this topic.

"Devolution of Technology" – August 31, 2022

Today the Lord is showing me (Kirk) His Church from His time on earth until the present. In particular, He wanted to show me what Satan has tried to do to it to destroy it. He showed me what He faced: the persecution by the religious, being tempted, and the division that was sown in His followers and His disciples. I saw His crucifixion. I saw how after the outpouring of the Holy Spirit, these things were intensified.

When Satan saw that this wasn't working, he tried to fold the church into the government, thinking that he would gain control over it and dispose of it through regulation and false promotion. When the church broke out of this scenario, Satan tried simple division based on intellectual knowledge of the scriptures (Denominations).

In these end times, Satan is using everything at his disposal, all of the above, and now technology as well. Through this technology, he accomplished a deception that could not have happened before. Yes, the entire planet has been deceived!

"But, I the Lord, declare that this tower of Babel will fall as surely as its namesake did!" (Jesus speaking.)

Then I see part animal/human/machine things made to replace humans and human laborers. These are to serve a few who would survive a series of events which would kill off most of the human race. The "humans" left on earth at this time would

115

be controlled by "elites" who are completely possessed by the demonic.

After I saw this, I said, "Lord, this is so depressing!"

Then He said, *"This last scenario will never happen, even though it is right on the cusp, right now. The 'knowledge' that produces these things is both earthly and demonic. I, the Lord, will not permit what I have created after My likeness and image to be re-created in the image of Satan and the demonic. And just as the Tower of Babel was deserted and went to ruin, so will this knowledge and technology be deserted and never will it be used again.*

I, the Lord, will cause a technology devolution to take place just as with the Tower of Babel. I have said that I would 'pull the plug' on artificial intelligence, and this is true. But this devolution will be way more extensive than that.

When the peoples of the earth see what had been planned for humankind and the earth as a whole, they will be completely undone! Museums will house the aberrations and tell of the atrocities on the earth, what had been planned, as well as how close to the precipice mankind had come! Such reckless use of technology will never again be permitted. Amen!"

"Time & Technology" – September 9, 2022

"Prophet, tell the people about time. A time to live, a time to die. What time is it? In your world your life revolves around time... a time to start and a time to stop. How long did you sleep? What did you do during this or that time in your life? Are you one who looks back in time, wishing for or desiring to live in times past? Or do you look forward, waiting for things

to happen, and desiring things to move faster? Do you actually live your life for Me or for time?

I created the environment in which you live, the mix of gases which you breathe, the water, plants, and animals, yes even time. The time it takes for the earth to make a revolution and the time for it to travel around the sun. In the beginning, I gave man dominion over his environment. He was to rule and reign over it. But he was deceived and fell to Satan in the garden. Under the rule of the evil one, he lost the dominion which I desired him to have. Because of My great love for those whom I had created, I won back dominion for them through the work of My Son, Jesus. I provided a way for those who would come to Him to be born again into the dominion I have always desired for them. Now Satan has been very successful in his deceit, and his lies have turned things around from what I desire for men.

He, Satan, is always after control. To rule and reign as I do. Can you see that everything that involves technology and invention has not served to make life better or easier for man, but instead has been used to enslave him? The promise of technology is always to make things better. Are things better? Or is mankind now being trained to serve technology? Who, or what, keeps track of where you are? What about your time, is it tracked and controlled by you? Are you 'off the clock' during your days, or are you always available? Technology is exerting more control in the lives of people faster than ever before, and this control is directly opposed to what I have desired for My people!

I have called the communication in the world 'The Tower of Babel,' for it represents one language, which is being used in rebellion against Me and My desires. And in fact, is one of

Satan's attempts to come against Me. I have also said that 'Where the Spirit of the Lord is, there is liberty, or freedom.' My Spirit has been poured out on the earth. Is there freedom? There will be! I, the Lord, have spoken!

My Son has said, 'The Spirit of the Lord is upon Me, Because He has anointed Me to preach the gospel to the poor. He has sent Me to proclaim release to the captives, And recovery of sight to the blind, To set free those who are oppressed, To proclaim the favorable year of the Lord.' My Son will not fail to deliver on all of these promises!

These earthly things that oppress My people will be walked back! Technology in the hands of a few will not be allowed to rule in My place! And NOW is the time that I will intervene to begin the devolution of this evil which is now in the world. Amen."

"Mastery Over All Technology by the Spirit" [AI, Quantum, etc.] – February 21, 2025

Partial prophetic word:

"... technology will never have the authority and power that comes from My Spirit. The realm of the spirit is reality itself, and I AM is King in this kingdom of the spirit. Therefore, no technology will ever have dominion in heaven or on earth, says the LORD. And My saints will learn what it really means to 'walk in the Spirit.' They will be creative, just as I AM is creative, and they will walk in Power and Authority over the created things and have mastery over even the most complex and powerful technology that can be imagined by man."

Besides having relevance because of what the Lord is prophesying in our lifetime, another reason Enoch's writings are increasingly important is because a lot more information regarding arch angels and fallen angels are included in the short writings of the Book of Enoch than what we find in most of the Bible. Since we are tasked with working with angels, it would be a good idea to know who the arch angels are, what their roles are, and how they interact with man, God, and each other.

Additionally, the Book of Enoch, also corroborates well with the information found in the Bible. Here are just a few examples:

1. **And the second voice I heard blessing the Elect One and the elect ones who hang upon the Lord of Spirits** (2:1:29). Father calls Jesus the Elect One in the original Greek in Luke 9:35. And those in Christ are often called elect throughout the New Testament.

2. **There I saw mansions of the elect and the mansions of the holy ...** (2:1:36a). Jesus told His disciples in His Father's house were many mansions and He was going there to prepare a place for them in John 14:1-6.

3. **This is the Son of Man who hath righteousness. With whom dwelleth righteousness, and who reveals all the treasures of that which is hidden...** (2:2:9). Paul records in Colossians 2:3 that all wisdom and knowledge are hidden in Christ. And Paul testifies in 1 Corinthians 1:30 that Jesus has become for us wisdom, righteousness, sanctification, and redemption.

4. **Yea, before the sun and the signs were created, before the stars of heaven were made, His name was named before the Lord of Spirits** (2:2:23). Paul testifies that Jesus is

before all things and in Him all things consist, having been created by Him (Colossians 1:15-17).

All of these reasons give us a good idea why it might be good for us to read the Book of Enoch. In the end, however, we are led by the Holy Spirit. If He leads you to read it, you should. If not, you shouldn't. And when you do read it, invite Him to read with you and reveal to you the truth.

Jesus said that eternal life was to know God and Jesus Christ whom He sent (John 17:3). He also said that His sheep hear His voice, they know Him, and they will not follow another shepherd (John 10:5, 14, 27).

As we stated in the introduction, this is the time for revealing and understanding the mysteries of God that have been hidden for centuries and millennia. It's the time of God's Great Reset where things hidden are being revealed, where things we've been deceived about are brought to the light, where lies are broken, truth is told, and justice prevails. It's the time when history books will be rewritten for those who desire to know the truth. It's the time where the great apostles of God arise and bring the revelation of Jesus Christ, with the help of their prophets, which is the foundation of the true church. It is the time for the Bride of Christ to be found without spot or wrinkle, to be truly washed by the water of the Word – the LORD Himself!

These end times are the times Enoch wrote about, the people he wrote to, and this is the time where the Church takes over all the mountains of influence in the world and brings the Lordship of Jesus Christ to the nations. Some call it the Millennial Reign. It's the time when the two witnesses in John's Revelation of Jesus Christ, the Apostles and Prophets who only follow the voice of the LORD, rise up and declare: **"The kingdoms of this world have become the Kingdoms of our LORD and of His Christ and He shall reign forever, and ever!"** (Revelation 11:15). Amen.

Bibliography

Marzulli, L. A., *On the Trail of the Nephilim*, Spiral of Life Publishing, 2013.

Marzulli, L. A., *On the Trail of the Nephilim II,* Spiral of Life Publishing, 2014.

Sanger, Laura, *The Roots of the Federal Reserve: Tracing the Nephilim from Noah to the U.S. Dollar,* Relentlessly Creative Books, LLC, 2020.

Winter, Dr. Jay. *The Complete Book of Enoch*, Winter Publications, 2015.

Author Biography

TIFFANY ROOT & KIRK VANDEGUCHTE bring Jesus to the nations through SGGM (Seeking the Glory of God Ministries). They have prophetic channels on YouTube and Rumble that can be found under Seeking the Glory of God, and they have devotionals on their SGGM DEVOTIONAL channels on YouTube and Rumble.

The Lord has said regarding SGGM (Seeking the Glory of God Ministries):

"The point of SGGM is to host a movement of the Spirit of God. In this 'model,' the fivefold ministry will be the government of the Church. Those who govern will be the servants of all, and they will not 'lord it over the congregants' as is done today.

This is a movement of disciples who go out. This is a movement where Jesus Christ is central and most importantly, where the Spirit of Christ is lifted high! In this movement, FAITH is spelled RISK and risk is spelled ACTION! Working for the Lord, in obedience to the Spirit is normal, and laziness and pew-sitting are very rare indeed.

'What church do you belong to?' This question will fade into the denomination era and will not be used anymore, at least not in the way it is now. People will either be members of The Universal Church, or not. And those who are Spirit-filled will know each other by the Spirit of God.

During this time, every prayer ever prayed for the Church will be fulfilled. All of the saints who ever desired to see a spotless bride for the Lord of All will see their prayers come to fruition during this time! Amen."

Other books in print can be found on Amazon.com.

Please visit www.sggm.world for more information.

www.ingramcontent.com/pod-product-compliance
Lightning Source LLC
Chambersburg PA
CBHW071836090426
42737CB00012B/2261